Minimum Wages—
Maximum Dignity

Minimum Wages— Maximum Dignity

A Manager's Guide to Affirming the Worth of All Employees

Brother Herman Zaccarelli, C.S.C.

iUniverse, Inc.
Bloomington

Minimum Wages—Maximum Dignity
A Manager's Guide to Affirming the Worth of All Employees

iUniverse books may be ordered through booksellers or by contacting:

iUniverse
1663 Liberty Drive
Bloomington, IN 47403
www.iuniverse.com
1-800-Authors (1-800-288-4677)

ISBN: 978-1-4620-1352-4 (sc)
ISBN: 978-1-4620-1353-1 (ebk)

Printed in the United States of America

iUniverse rev. date: 06/13/2011

Table of Contents

Section 1. Recognizing the Valuable Contribution of Lower-waged Workers

1. To Customers 3
2. To Their Work Team 8
3. To Their Supervisor 14
4. To Their Community 20

Section 2. Affirming the Dignity of Each Employee

1. Concerning Economic Status 29
2. Concerning Ethnicity 35
3. Concerning Parenthood 41
4. Concerning Diversity 48

Section 3. Assisting With Training and Education

1. Committing to On-the-Job Training 57
2. Implementing On-the-Job Training and Education ... 63
3. Creating Career Ladders 69
4. Aiding in Off-Site Educational Opportunities 75

Section 4. Improving Workers' Health

1.   Recognizing the Impact of Health on Productivity.................   83
2.   Ensuring Safety on the Job..   89
3.   Addressing Healthy Eating...   95
4.   Accessing Public Assistance Programs..............................   100

Section 5. Enhancing the Lives of Workers' Families

1.   Food Assistance   109
2.   Child Care (daycare) Assistance   116
3.   Accessing Housing Options   122
4.   Supporting Local School Systems   127

DEDICATION

Minimum Wages—Maximum Dignity: A Manager's Guide To Affirming The Worth Of All Employees is dedicated to the thousands of hard-working hourly-paid workers I have come to know in my years of service to the hospitality and foodservice industries.

This is the 60th Anniversary of taking my religious vows in the congregation of Holy Cross. I am extremely grateful to all of the Brothers and Priests who encouraged and sustained me through these very joyful years. This book is also for them.

America's working poor face real challenges in how they are viewed at work and often in how they view themselves. In most cases, lower-waged workers have little power to change the circumstances they encounter at work.

So this book is most importantly dedicated to those managers who *do* have that power, and the desire, to transform the lives of their lower-waged employees for the better. My hope for them is that they have the understanding, the compassion, and most of all the courageous will . . . to do just that.

Brother Herman Zaccarelli, C.S.C.
Cocoa Beach, Florida

FORWARD

While it is a fact that the wage rates paid to workers in many lower-waged jobs are low and will likely remain low; it is also true that managers and supervisors in all segments of today's economy have an extraordinary opportunity to demonstrate to these workers that their value is high.

Managers and supervisors can have this impact because the economic world we live in is the direct result of our own actions; not the inevitability of mysterious market forces.

In most cases, America's low-wage workers have limited power to change their working conditions, but that limitation is not at all mysterious. Rather it is the direct result of a series of political, economic and corporate decisions made by real people. And real people have the ability to change the lives of lower-waged workers for the better; . . . if they choose to do so.

In each of the 20 important sections contained in *Minimum Wage—Maximum Dignity: A Manager's Guide to Affirming the Worth of All Employees,* Brother Herman points out a significant truth about the working poor . . . and about ourselves. He then clearly shows, using real-life work examples, how those truths directly affect lower-waged workers and the organizations that employ them.

To meet the myriad challenges faced by lower-waged workers, over 100 practical low-cost or no-cost examples of positive, value-affirming actions that can be taken by managers and supervisors are presented in this book. To conclude each important section, Brother Herman clearly addresses the impact these affirming actions will have on lower-waged workers . . . and those organizations that employ them.

Those who feel minimum-waged workers are unjustly paid will find no exhortations to radically alter these workers pay scales. Rather, the book focuses on what can be done now to radically alter these worker's lives.

Similarly, those who feel minimum-waged and lower-waged workers are already fairly paid may be surprised to discover the strong business case that can be made for treating them even more fairly.

Perhaps the most magical power of *Minimum Wages—Maximum Dignity: A Manager's Guide to Affirming The Worth of All Employees*, however, lies in its consistent message that those who have the desire, and the compassionate will, to positively transform the lives of their lower-waged workers will inevitably transform their own in the same powerful way.

David K. Hayes, Ph.D. and Peggy A. Hayes
Panda Professionals Hospitality Management and Training
Okemos, MI

INTRODUCTION

Doing the Right Thing IS the Right Thing to Do

This book was written to identify specific low-cost or no-cost steps that pragmatic, yet enlightened, employers can take to affirm the value and enhance the self-worth of their lower-waged employees.

It is a reality of today's economy that much of the work done each day is assigned to workers who have limited skills, limited education, or both. The lower pay of these workers reflects those limitations. It is essential to understand, however, that while their pay may be low, their importance, and the importance of their work, is very high.

Food service workers, hotel room attendants, cashiers in retail stores, grocery store stockers, janitorial services workers, child care workers, office cleaners, lawn care providers, health care aides, and farm workers are just a few examples of the myriad groups of employees who daily perform tasks that are of critical significance to those they serve, as well as to the efficient operation of our economy and the betterment of all our lives.

In the best of worlds, perhaps, these essential workers would immediately receive pay raises that would allow them to readily achieve the dreams they have for themselves and to meet the aspirations they have for their families. The reality for these workers, however, is that due to economic practicality most will not receive significant increases in pay. If they stay in their jobs they will, in many cases, remain in the same lower-scale pay ranges. Just or unjust; lower-waged workers are a fixture in the fabric of every nation's economy.

It would be easy to write a book filled with appeals, supplications, or even demands to increase the wages of these lower-paid workers. This is not that book. Rather, this book assumes its readers are currently paying their employees hourly wages that are in keeping with these workers' skills and job assignments. But it assumes more. It assumes its readers are leaders; leaders who know they can *do more* to benefit their employees and their own organizations.

While it is true that even the most considerate of employers may not be in a position to significantly alter the pay structure of their lowest-paid workers, it is just as true that they can, without question, do a great deal to improve the lives of these workers and their families.

This book identifies five key actions that are the right things to do to make a positive difference in the lives of workers as well as impact the success of the organizations employing them. These are:

> ➤ Recognizing the Valuable Contribution of Lower-wage Workers
> ➤ Affirming the Dignity of Each Worker
> ➤ Assisting With Training and Education
> ➤ Improving Workers' Health
> ➤ Enhancing the Lives of Workers' Families

In each of these key areas the specific reasons *why* managers should get involved, *what* they can do, and the *results* they can expect are directly addressed.

Doing the right things for their employees is, of course, the virtuous thing to do. But this book also shows why it the *right* thing to do; for all those employers who understandably must be just as concerned with the success of their bottom lines as with the success of their lower paid workers. Fortunately, for businesses and workers, these dual concerns are inextricably connected. Success in both can be achieved by utilizing many of the low-cost or no-cost management activities identified in this book.

SECTION 1

Recognizing the Valuable Contribution of Lower-waged Workers

To Customers

What You Know

In America, what you *do* is often seen as a powerful statement about who you are.

That's not necessarily bad, or good. It simply is. In your own job, much of the satisfaction you feel likely results from your own sense of accomplishment. That's why surveys consistently show that those in professions that involve doing creative work or helping others describe themselves as happier at work than those who have a harder time seeing the direct impact of what they do.

Everyone who works wants to feel they make a real difference; in the lives of others, their families and their own. If you think about how you feel about your own job, you'll agree that's true.

Lower-paid workers naturally feel the same way about their jobs. Pay is not a primary source of feelings of self-worth for most of them simply because their jobs do not readily afford them that source of motivation. But they do have the same need you have; to feel good about themselves and most importantly, about what they do each day at work.

As a successful manager, you know the importance of a sense of purpose at work. For you, it's likely conceiving, and then achieving, the vision you have created for your work team. Your minimum wage employees seek that same sense of purpose. It's up to you to first recognize the value of your employees to those you serve and to then communicate clearly to your employees the importance of those contributions. It takes effort, and it's worth it!

Addressing this key need to affirm the value of who they are; through what they do and who they serve, is an activity that you can and should undertake for their benefit and for your own.

WHY IT COUNTS

"Why are you leaving", asked Tamara, a day-shift waitress at Owen's family restaurant. "The tips are just as good here as they will be at the Pancake House."

Tamara was talking to Lena, her friend and co-server at Owen's.

Lena had just confided to Tamara that she had accepted a job starting next week at a restaurant that was a direct competitor of Owen's.

"I know," replied Lena, "the pays the same, but when I talked to them they really made me feel like they needed me. And that I could make a difference over there. I'm not sure our boss here will even notice when I'm gone."

"Well, I don't know about that," said Tamara, "but it's sure gonna be different not having you here. You're our best server!"

1. How do you think customers at Owen's will be affected when Tamara leaves? _____

2. How do you think Tamara's supervisor at Owen's will be affected by her leaving? _____

3. Do you think Tamara left Owen's for a better job? _____

What To Do

Review the suggested low-cost activities below to determine if your own employees would benefit from them. If so, identify a target date for their implementation, then follow up to document your completion of the activity.

Suggested Management Activity	Target Date	Completion Date
Schedule 15 minutes each week to visit with your lower-waged workers. Share organizational successes and goals so they continually stay involved in the vision. This can be done by staff meetings, a morning donut and coffee get-together, an afternoon cookie break, or whatever creative way you can strategically connect, motivate, and praise your staff.	____/____	____/____

• At least once per quarter, hold private, closed door meetings with each lower-waged employee to clearly explain the importance of their individual efforts to

the specific internal or external audiences
your work group serves.   ____/____   ____/____

- At least twice per year hold private, closed
  door meetings with each lower-waged
  employee to personally thank them for a
  specific and positive aspect of their work
  performance. Examples could include good
  attendance, punctuality, and adherence
  to dress code requirements or attitude
  toward customers. Find the positive in each
  employee and make your appreciation know
  to them.   ____/____   ____/____

- Annually send a holiday card to the home
  address of each employee with a personal
  (and handwritten) note from you affirming
  the employee's importance to the success
  of your organization. Recognize that these
  cards will be proudly displayed at the homes
  of many of your lower-waged workers.   ____/____   ____/____

- Regularly plan mini-celebrations at work to
  recognize significant employee milestones;
  e.g. 1 year anniversary, 5 year anniversary,
  promotion, and the like. During the
  celebration emphasize to all employees
  the importance to your organization of
  loyalty and longevity. Demonstrate your
  appreciation with a modestly priced pin, gift
  or other appropriate work place reward.   ____/____   ____/____

WHY IT WORKS

✓ **For Your Employees**
Everyone wants to know their efforts at work have meaning and are valued. Knowing that helps affirm an individual's self-worth and respect. As well, everyone wants to feel truly appreciated by those who benefit from their efforts and to see that appreciation put into words and action. When they do, their response is overwhelmingly positive.

✓ **For You and Your Organization**
As a manager you know the good feelings and improved work attitude that result when your own boss recognizes your positive efforts and sincerely demonstrates his or her appreciation for your hard work. Those same positive feelings that help propel you to do your best are present in your lower-waged workers and when you tap into them you unleash a powerful motivator.

Take It Away

> *"I laugh, I love, I hope, I try, I hurt, I need, I fear, I cry.*
> *And I know you do the same things too;*
> *So we're really not that different, me and you."*
>
> *Colin Raye*

To Their Work Team

What You Know

Even though you may instantly recognize the song from the music video "We Are the World" when you hear it, you may not know that it is one of only thirty all-time single song releases that have gone on to sell over 10,000,000 copies. That's not so surprising when you recognize that the artists who worked on writing or singing the song included such famous performers as Michael Jackson, Lionel Richie, Stevie Wonder, Ray Charles, Billie Joel, Diana Ross, Bruce Springsteen and Smokey Robinson among many others.

"We Are the World" was written and performed to raise money for famine relief in Africa and it was extraordinarily successful. What may be most remarkable of all, however, is how a large number of incredibly talented individual performers came together as a *team*. While each of these stars contributed to the song; each did not perform a solo in the song. They understood their own roles and the importance of teamwork to the success of the collective effort.

Those who truly understand the music business, however, also know that for every well-known star contributing to the success of this song, there was a multitude of critical behind-the scenes support staff contributing to their efforts. These sound technicians, make-up artists, lighting specialists, electricians, meal providers and others like them also played critical roles in creating the finished product that became "We Are the World."

Like you, your lower-waged workers also want to understand how their individual efforts fit into the larger picture of achieving your organization's goals. Often, it is not readily apparent to these employees exactly how their actions impact other workers within the organization.

As a manager you know that the work of one employee often directly affects the ability of another to complete his or her own job. Because that is true, helping your lower-waged employees better understand how their individual contributions affect the work of others is an important part of leading your work team. It increases your team members' self-esteem and understanding when they recognize they are making an important contribution to something larger than what they can readily see.

WHY IT COUNTS

"Well, I've just been to the third floor and you've done it again," said Tyrell, the General Manager of the 300-room Carlton Suites hotel.

"Done what?," asked Maria, a laundry worker in the hotel's housekeeping department, "Am I in trouble?"

Tyrell Jackson was in the laundry room, in the basement of the hotel, and was talking to Maria. Her job was to carefully fold the bath mats, bath towels, hand towels and wash cloths required to stock the housekeeping carts used by room attendants working on each of the hotel's nine floors.

"Not at all," replied Tyrell with a smile, "in fact I just wanted to stop down here to tell you that you are doing a great job making sure all of the items you fold are folded to the right size. That makes it easier for the room attendants to stock their carts with enough clean towels to clean their assigned rooms quickly. And that means our guests all get their rooms cleaned faster. It really means a lot to all of them. And to me!"

1. Does knowing that your job directly affects others in your organization help inspire you to do your best work? _____

2. How do you think Tyrell's comments will affect how Maria views the importance of her job to the efforts of the Housekeeping team at the hotel?

3. How do you think the hotel's future guests will be directly affected by Maria's better understanding of her critical role on the housekeeping team?

What To Do

Review the suggested low-cost activities below to determine if your own employees would benefit from them. If so, identify a target date for their implementation, then follow up to document your completion of the activity.

	Target Date	Completion Date
Suggested Management Activity		

- Consider each of your lower-waged workers. Think through what would happen if any one of them did not perform their tasks for a day. Who in your organization would be affected and how? Take five minutes and make it a point to let the person you were thinking about know exactly how important their work is to others in your organization. ____/____ ____/____

- Consider each of your lower-waged workers. Think through what would happen if any one of them did not perform their task for a day. How would the customers served by your organization be affected? Take five minutes and make it a point to let the person you were thinking about know exactly how important their work is to the customers served by your organization. ____/____ ____/____

- Review your new employee orientation checklist to ensure you include directly addressing with newly hired lower-waged workers that they are 1.) Joining a winning team; that 2.) The expectations for team members are high and that 3.) They should feel very proud to have been selected to join the team. ____/____ ____/____

- Quarterly, hold a short cross-functional team meeting with lower-waged workers to explain how the work of each group directly affects the performance of the other team members.   ____/____   ____/____

- Plan and implement an annual team building event for after-work hours (e.g. attending a sports event or local festival, a meal, or an afternoon trip to a coffeehouse). During the event emphasize the importance of teamwork to the success of your team.   ____/____   ____/____

WHY IT WORKS

✓ **For Your Employees**
Lower-waged earners often struggle against the negative stigmas that come with their positions. Improving self-esteem and a sense of appreciation are essential. Emphasizing teamwork can help change employee attitudes and instill a sense of pride and enjoyment in accomplishing the group's goals.

✓ **For You and Your Organization**
Understanding the value of all your employees and succeeding in motivating them to operate as a team improves the workplace environment, builds strong relationships among them, and can inspire ever greater team accomplishments.

Take It Away

"Teamwork is no accident. It is the by-product of good leadership."

John Adair

To Their Supervisor

What You Know

Did you ever notice that children continually seek parental recognition to validate their actions?

"Watch me, Mom!" is likely one of the most common phrases a mother hears from her child. Children want their parents to "see" what they can do. This need also explains the parental wisdom of using the front of the refrigerator as an art gallery; regardless of the quality of their youngsters' artistic efforts!

Actually, when you observe them closely you quickly find that there is little a child does that is not motivated and enhanced by their parent's recognition and approval of the activity. In fact, parents of little ones know that they quickly lose interest in what they are doing if they are not being noticed and praised for it.

It is a curious and fascinating aspect of human behavior that we don't really outgrow this need as we mature. For most of us, the need to gain the approval of those closest to us remains unchanged our entire lives. And, in fact, psychologists tell us that the more unsure a person is of his or her inherent worth or ability, the more reassurance and praise they need.

Lower wage positions often do not come with the societal symbols of personal achievement that publicly validate self-worth or material success. It is not surprising then that workers in these positions especially want and benefit from others' approval and appreciation.

Just as involved parents spend a large part of their time watching and admiring the actions of their children, a good manager needs to make plenty of time for praise and recognition of their staff. That's because lower-waged workers are a lot like you; they are all grown up, but they retain the same desire to gain the acceptance and admiration of those they respect and who they feel are important in their lives and their success. As their supervisor, that's you!

In large measure, the pride they feel in themselves, and put into their work, will be a reflection of the pride you show in them.

WHY IT COUNTS

"Nice job Jason, that looks great;" said Laura as she and Dan walked through the salad dressing section of the Speedway supermarket.

Laura was the store manager at the Speedway. Dan was new and had recently been hired to be a supervisor in the grocery and dry goods section of the store. It was 4:00 a.m. and Laura was touring the aisles with Dan while the store was being re-stocked by the night crew.

"Thanks," replied Jason with big smile.

"You do that a lot," said Dan as hc and Laura left the aisle where Jason was re-stocking shelves, carefully rotating stock and meticulously placing the new product on the shelves with the labels facing out.

"Do what?" asked Laura.

"Use the hourly employee's name when you compliment their work," replied Dan.

"That's true," said Laura pausing to look at Dan, "Dale Carnegie once said that a person's name is, to them, the sweetest most important sound in any language. Do you agree . . . Dan?"

1. How do you think Jason feels about being singled out for praise by the store's General Manager? _____

2. Do you agree with Carnegie that when you use a person's name in conversation with him or her, it makes a difference in how that person feels about themselves, and about you? _____

3. Do you think Dan is likely to model his own employee-related praise giving actions based on what he has seen Laura do? _____ Why? _____

What To Do

Review the suggested low-cost activities below to determine if your own employees would benefit from them. If so, identify a target date for their implementation, then follow up to document your completion of the activity.

Suggested Management Activity	**Target Date**	**Completion Date**
• Implement an employee recognition program (e.g. Employee of the Month, Associate of the Quarter, or similar program) that makes sense for your organization. Reward the winner with a token of appreciation from your organization and publicly recognize the winners.	____/____	____/____
• Know your employees' names. Schedule at least 15 minutes per week to make "How's it going?" rounds with your lower-waged workers. Complement positive aspects of their work and remember to use their names in conversation with them.	____/____	____/____
• Invite family members of employees to the workplace for a tour and/or sample of the product you produce or the service you provide. Be sure to emphasize the importance, to your entire organization, of		

the work being done by the employee whose family is touring. ____/____   ____/____

• Arrange, at least quarterly, a group meeting / celebration where a specific part of the agenda is to publicly recognize each lower-waged worker and to comment positively on one aspect of his or her contribution to the work group's effort. ____/____   ____/____

• On a regular basis (i.e. monthly or quarterly) give prizes of modest cost to employees that publicly reward them for good performance. For example, rewards for good attendance, punctuality, adherence to dress code, friendliness, or positive attitude toward customers. ____/____   ____/____

WHY IT WORKS

✓ **For Your Employees**
People are hard wired for praise and approval. It's often how we define ourselves. If what we "do" is socially admirable (e.g. doctor, CEO, famous athlete, celebrity), then our work itself most often serves to satisfy our need for acceptance. But, if what we "do" is not inherently perceived by ourselves or others as quite so socially significant (e.g., room cleaner, dishwasher, stocker, cashier, fry cook, grass cutter), then individual recognition from their supervisors is much needed, much sought after and much appreciated.

✓ **For You and Your Organization**

Providing praise and recognition to lower-waged workers is simple. It's low-cost; often no-cost and extremely powerful. But most importantly, the results are instant, consistent and highly effective. In addition to the immense value it brings to employees, you will be a better manager for it as well. That's because displaying a positive attitude toward your workers improves teamwork; and your own level of success!

Take It Away

> *"Appreciate everything your associates do for the business. Nothing else can quite substitute for a few well-chosen, well-timed, sincere words of praise. They're absolutely free and worth a fortune."*
>
> *Sam Walton: Founder, Wal-Mart*

To Their Community

What You Know

Instincts and insightful perceptions help protect us. It's common practice in our society to evaluate and categorize the people we see, the activities we participate in, the quality of the products we buy, the risks of our environment, the food we eat; . . . virtually everything. The thoughtful assessment of what we observe each day serves a useful purpose because it helps us make sense of our surroundings and function appropriately.

Unfortunately, however, an all-to-common by-product of this process can be that we become judgmental and unfairly biased. Just as our perceptions of what we "see" in the world can be accurate, they can also be incorrect. When that happens, our view of the world can be distorted by our own prejudices.

Your lower-waged employees may suffer from a stigma created by working in an environment or for a company that triggers a negative perception in their communities. When that is the case, it can be incredibly difficult for them to change how they are viewed by others. It can also be highly discouraging to consistently cope with the disrespect and disregard for their work that they may encounter.

As a manager of lower-waged hourly workers, you may not be able to change the world's perception of the work your employees do, but you can affect the impact of that perception on your employees. You can help do that by creating and sharing a vision of their work that is larger than their workplace.

When you think about it, you immediately recognize the benefits to society and to families, of its members simply holding down a responsible job. Workers who do just that form the foundation of their communities. They support themselves, take care of their children, pay taxes for local schools, support local businesses, fund local churches, contribute to charities, and are able to donate some of their time for any number of good causes. Without these individuals' efforts, businesses and communities crumble.

Productive work, at all pay levels, has a positive impact on the quality of neighborhoods, communities, society, and everyone's collective prosperity. Workers at all levels play an important role in their local communities, and these roles are deserving of great respect. It is part of your job to communicate that fact to your staff at all levels of your organization; . . . and especially to those doing work the outside world may erroneously perceive as demeaning.

WHY IT COUNTS

"I'm not stupid;" said Kellena Martin to Tony Yabbara.

Tony was Kellena's supervisor at the Dollar House, where Kellena worked as one of the check-out cashiers. The Dollar House sold a variety of merchandise. The store was very popular and almost always very busy.

Tony couldn't tell if Kellena was about to cry or about to kick the door to the office where they were meeting. Either way, he could tell she was upset.

The problem had started when a customer Kellena was checking out of the store had demanded to see the manager. The customer's debit card was rejected by the store's computerized payment system and as Kellena had tried to explain that to her, the customer became increasingly agitated and demanded to see the manager.

When Tony arrived at the check-out counter to address the guest's issue, he asked what he could do to assist. The customer had immediately replied, "Well, you might start by firing the employees you have who are too stupid to process a simple credit card transaction."

It was at that point that Tony had asked Kellena to go to the office and wait for him.

After finishing with the customer, Tony had entered the office to find a still visibly upset Kellena.

"I know that;" replied Tony to Kellena's opening comment. "I also know that there are lots of business people who like to say that the customer is always right. Well . . . . they aren't! And we need to talk."

1. How important to her self-esteem do you think Tony's genuine support and concern for Kellena will be in this situation? _____
2. How important to the other cashiers at the Dollar House would be hearing about their manager's insistence that customers not be allowed to demean or abuse any of the store's lower-waged employees? _____

3. Do you think insensitive and inaccurate comments similar to the one made by the customer in this scenario are common occurrences in the lives of lower-waged workers you employ? _____

What To Do

Review the suggested low-cost activities below to determine if your own employees would benefit from them. If so, identify a target date for their implementation, then follow up to document your completion of the activity.

Suggested Management Activity	Target Date	Completion Date
• Develop and strictly enforce a "zero tolerance" policy regarding abusive language or behavior directed by customers or co-workers toward lower-waged employees.	____/____	____/____
• Make it a point to emphasize your own commitment to community by modeling behavior that shows your self-worth is based on more than just your at-the-job activities.	____/____	____/____
• Create a work environment where you emphasize that character is as valuable as the job duties performed by employees. Publicly recognize and praise outstanding character among your lower-paid workers		

as often as you recognize and praise their
job performance.   _____/_____   _____/_____

- Make your workgroup an example of
  good character and citizenship by actively
  involving your business and lower-waged
  workers in your local community's
  philanthropic activities (e.g. community
  clean-up days, workplace charity drives,
  adopt a family for Thanksgiving programs,
  Toys-for Tots, or winter coat collection
  drives, and the like.)   _____/_____   _____/_____

- Annually, review all of your written
  policies and procedures to ensure each
  will make a positive impact on worker
  self-esteem. If any do not, discuss these
  with your lower-waged workers and with
  other supervisors in your organizations
  to determine positive ways in which these
  policies can be revised.   _____/_____   _____/_____

WHY IT WORKS

✓ **For Your Employees**
Making a living is not making a life.
Because of the perceptions of others (and often their own) many of your
lower-waged workers cannot rely on their vocation to provide them with high
levels of self-esteem, motivation, or self-satisfaction. This is because, fairly
or unfairly, the work they do, and positions they hold may be seen by others

as actually detracting from their stature. Therefore, it is crucial that you help these workers understand and experience the empowerment that comes from recognizing their self-worth is developed through character, personal relationships and commitment to community; not just the tasks they perform while at work.

✓ **For You and Your Organization**

As a manager, it's easy to begin to feel that your vocation is synonymous with your life. Sometimes it truly feels that way! It's important for you, however; and for employees at all levels of your organization, to remember the significance of character, citizenship and relationships to a healthy and satisfying life. When you reflect regularly on your own responsibility to family and community, and emphasize its importance to your lower-waged workers, you directly affect your own feelings of happiness, value and self-worth, as well as theirs.

Take It Away

"To surround yourself with the things and the people that make you happy in life; . . . this is success."

Sasha Azevedo

SECTION 2

Affirming the Dignity of Each Employee

Concerning Economic Status

What You Know

A recent winner of the popular American television show, "American Idol" said the following while speaking to the public about her triumph; *"If you work hard enough, and don't give up, you can reach your dreams just like I did."* It sounds good, but the reality is that in the year she won the competition over 100,000 other contestants also tried to reach their dream along with her; but failed to do so.

Many wanted it just as much. Many tried just as hard.

But there are numerous factors involved in reaching the "top" and the space is limited. Is it possible to get there with hard work alone? Usually not. In this case it took tens of millions of people voting for this person's success before she won. The other 100,000 Idol contestants went right back to their previous jobs. The ones they too were hoping to leave behind.

In the United States, over 40 million jobs—or about one in three—pay low wages. The great majority of these low-wage jobs lack benefits such as health insurance or retirement accounts and, in many cases, provide little or no chance for career advancement. These conditions translate into millions of Americans who earn poverty-level incomes, while millions more struggle to make ends meet. Who are the working poor? We often know them best by the jobs they hold. These include:

Agricultural equipment operators	Hotel and motel desk clerks
Baggage porters/bellhops	Janitors and cleaners
Bartenders	Hotel laundry workers
Call center workers	Dry-cleaning workers
Cashiers	Locker room attendants
Child-care workers	Maids and housekeepers
Cooks (fast food)	Manicurists and pedicurists
Crossing guards	Nonfarm animal caretakers
Counter and rental clerks	Nurse's aides
Dining room attendants (bussers)	Parking lot attendants
Dishwashers	Retail salespeople
Education assistants	Security guards
Farm labor contractors	Service station attendants
Farm workers	Sewing machine operators
Food preparation workers	Carpet shampooers
Funeral attendants	Taxi drivers and chauffeurs
Hand packers and packagers	Theater ushers (ticket takers)
Home health aides	Waiters and waitresses

Given the uniquely American view that if people are simply industrious enough they will inevitably be successful in life leaves many to conclude therefore, that being a low wage earner means a person must be lazy, stupid, unskilled, unmotivated or something similar. And because of that, they are "lucky" to have a job.

The reality is that most low wage earners are often anything but lucky economically. And a great majority of them work harder than any person in a more skilled position is required to work. In many cases that means they don't have the time or the financial resources needed to acquire more education or training. They aren't generally eligible for significant career advancement, increased benefits, or wages no matter how hard they work or good a job they do. And many work two jobs just to get by. They certainly aren't lazy. And, they certainly deserve a break.

You can be the one to give them that.

WHY IT COUNTS

"Look Jana, I'm sorry Lori called in sick, but she did. That's why I need you to work extra for us today" said Joseph Pearson, the supervisor at Littleton Industries, and Jana Foster's boss.

Jana worked on the mail line at Littleton and she, along with her friend Lori and five others, worked the third shift' from 11:00 p.m. to 7:00 a.m. four days per week, packing Littleton products for shipping to its customers world-wide.

"I would Joe," replied Jana, "but I have to be to work at my other job at 8:00 this morning. You know I only get 32 hours a week here, so I have to work two jobs. If I don't show up there on time I'll lose that job. I was careful to make sure they only scheduled me this week when I wasn't on the schedule here."

"But I need you here today," replied Joseph, "you need to get your priorities straight or I can't guarantee you you'll be on my schedule next week!"

1. Joseph wants Jana to get her priorities straight. What are Jana's priorities?

   _____

   _____

2. What would you do if you were Jana? _____

   _____

3. What would you advise Joseph to do if Jana decides to go to her other job?

   _____

   If she doesn't go? _____

What To Do

Review the suggested low-cost activities below to determine if your own employees would benefit from them. If so, identify a target date for their implementation, then follow up to document your completion of the activity.

Suggested Management Activity	Target Date	Completion Date
• Be aware of how physically and mentally draining some of your positions may be and counter that whenever possible. Offer a comfortable and pleasant work environment. Schedule necessary breaks and change routines. Play music, have fun.	____/____	____/____
• Listen and take action. Take time to know your employees' goals and dreams. Find out if there are ways that you can help them overcome some of their obstacles.	____/____	____/____

- Ask employees directly about their outside employment. Use this information when determining work schedules. Ensure your lower-waged workers know that you recognize the economic necessity of multiple jobs they may hold and assure them that your organization will be fair and reasonable with policies that could affect accommodating their outside work schedules   ____/____   ____/____

- Many lower-wage workers have jobs that start and stop at specific times. But many working professionals take for granted that they can leave the office for a couple of hours to go to the dentist, a parent-teacher conference, or to take an elderly parent to the doctor. At least quarterly, review your policies and then meet with other department supervisors to identify ways to allow lower-waged workers some of the same type of flexibility.   ____/____   ____/____

- Use whatever advantages you've been blessed with (good health, education and skills) to actively assist those who can benefit from your knowledge and talents.   ____/____   ____/____

WHY IT WORKS

✓ **For Your Employees**

Every person has a story. Every person has a dream. It is rare when just hard work alone gets you to where you want to be. Most people who succeed have had lots of help along the way. It all starts with somebody taking the time to reach out a helping hand.

✓ **For You and Your Organization**

It's true that not all of your workers may be worth a big investment of your time. But taking the time to find out which ones are, and then helping them succeed at whatever level they can is time well spent. Creating strength at every level helps build an organization that is vibrant and whose potential, like some lower-waged workers, is unlimited.

Take It Away

"There is no such thing as a 'self-made' man.
We are made up of thousands of others.
Everyone who has ever done a kind deed for us, or spoken one word of encouragement to us, has entered into the make-up of our character and of our thoughts; as well as our success."

George Matthew Adams

Concerning Ethnicity

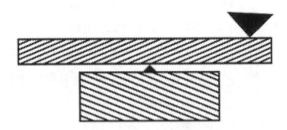

You may think these rectangles are tilted; the truth is that the horizontal lines in this diagram are all parallel.

What we think we see (our perceptions) are not always reliable.

What You Know

What comes to mind when you hear the phrase "race relations?"

Unfortunately, for many people, it immediately conjures up images that are pretty similar to those that come to mind when a college football fan hears the words "arch rival."

The emotional reaction is strong, and in many cases, not always positive. Thoughts of arch rivals can result in the formation of a subconscious "Us" vs. "Them" mentality. Who are these "Other Guys?" For some Whites it might be Blacks, for some Blacks it might be Whites, but there is usually plenty of rivalry, based on unfounded prejudice, to go around.

Just like in college football, it seems some people actually need a group of "Thems" to root against. The "Them" groups usually change over time, but at the time this book is being written, it's Hispanics and Muslims who are in the societal hot seat in America.

The predictable result is often loud and angry debate about such emotional political issues as immigration reform and the citizenship status of the children of illegal aliens (today's Hispanic issues) and the right to build churches or wear religion-influenced dress while on the job (today's Muslim issues).

It's pretty clear that when it comes to ethnic and cultural differences, "Us" vs. "Them" attitudes can often result in misunderstanding and injustice. That's true whether we get our information from Fox news or from MSNBC. It's often easy to believe and even react to opinions that seek to pit "Us" against "Them."

The reality, of course, is that you know each of us has much more in common than not; especially at work. As a manager, when you recognize that a team made of "Us" always includes "Them", the prejudices held toward any group, and especially the lower-waged workers that may at first seem so different from us, and from each other, melt away.

It's unlikely that you, regardless of your good intentions, can eliminate all of the subtle prejudice or outright racism you may observe toward and or even among your lower-waged workers. But, when you recognize your ability to act, to make a difference right this moment, to do what you can do to ensure equality on the job for all of your lower-waged workers you can help make justice and fairness a reality in your own workplace.

WHY IT COUNTS

"Good morning," said Nora, the supervisor of cleaning crews for Potter's Janitorial Services.

Nora had just arrived at work on Thursday morning to find Jesse, Larry and Art, all members of the janitorial crew, chatting in the supplies area as they prepared to stock their cleaning vans for the day's work assignments.

"Larry bowled a 250 last night!" said Art excitedly.

Trish knew that Jesse, Larry, Art and some other members of her 40-person crew were in a Wednesday night bowling league. She also knew that no women, Blacks or Hispanics had been invited to join them.

"Sounds like fun," said Nora. "I would think some of the other guys and gals here might like it too. Have you asked them?

"No, we haven't," said Larry warily, "Look, it's just us guys. We just hang out."

"But not with everyone. Right?" said Nora.

"Come on," replied Henry, "that's not fair. We aren't wearing white sheets. And we aren't hurting anyone. We're just more comfortable bowling with other guys just like us. And besides, we're not at work. It's our free time."

1. Assume you were a Hispanic, Black or female working at Potters. How would you feel about the bowling league? _____
2. Blatant racism in the work place is pretty much a thing of the past, however, subtle forms of racism still happen on and off the job and they can directly affect worker cohesiveness. What do you think would cause one group of

workers to feel that only members of their own group are "<u>just like us</u>"; while others are not? _____

3. Would you advise Nora to take steps to promote cohesiveness among different ethnic and gender groups at Potter's? _____
What do you think will happen in the future if she doesn't act? _____

_____

What To Do

Review the suggested low-cost activities below to determine if your own employees would benefit from them. If so, identify a target date for their implementation, then follow up to document your completion of the activity.

Suggested Management Activity	**Target Date**	**Completion Date**
• Be colorblind. Look for the character inside your workers, not their color on the outside.	____/____	____/____
• Ensure by your own leadership and actions that all employees are treated equally and respectfully by co-workers, customers.	____/____	____/____
• Work actively to foster a sense of inclusivity, not exclusivity, by helping to dispel negative images and false perceptions about members of your work team.	____/____	____/____
• Actively acknowledge accomplishments made by famous/public figures from the		

same ethnic backgrounds as your work
group.

____/____   ____/____

- On a regular basis take the opportunity
to stress your team's commonalities
by arranging for members of *different*
sub-groups to come together to participate
in work-related problem solving activities.

____/____   ____/____

WHY IT WORKS

✓ **For Your Employees**
Skin color is permanent. Genetics and family history are unchangeable. These
are significant influences but a lot more than what can be seen on the outside
is contained on the inside. Everyone deserves a chance to be seen for who they
really are, not merely who they appear to be.

✓ **For You and Your Organization**
Working effectively with groups of people requires finesse. Emotions and
interactions can be explosive between groups and the results can be rivalry and
tension. When people relate to each other as individuals, however, they are
much more likely to be friendly and work well together. Your work team will be
more productive when any tensions related to an "Us" vs. "Them" mentality are
eliminated. That starts with you.

Take It Away

"I have a dream that my four little children will one day live in a nation where they will not be judged by the color of their skin, but by the content of their character."

Dr. Martin Luther King

Concerning Parenthood

What You Know

As a manger you are often faced with making a decision that includes two or more choices. Your task is to select the "best" choice. But what do you do if neither choice can really be considered best?

That's the dilemma facing working poor parents who must decide between staying home to care for a sick child, (and losing the income they desperately need . . . as well as putting their job at risk) or going to work (and leaving their child unattended).

Given those two unattractive choices, it's no surprise what most parents choose. And those choices can hurt your business. *"I can't come in today because my child is sick"* and *"I can't come in today because my babysitter is sick"* are words that every supervisor of lower-paid working moms and dads has heard all too often.

To make matters even worse, in the United States only 46 percent of working parents with incomes below the poverty line have access to any paid leave. This includes paid sick leave, paid vacation, or paid personal days. But over 80 percent of working parents with incomes over 200 percent of the poverty level have access to paid leave. Without access to paid leave, personal illness or a sick child can present serious economic difficulties for lower-income working parents.

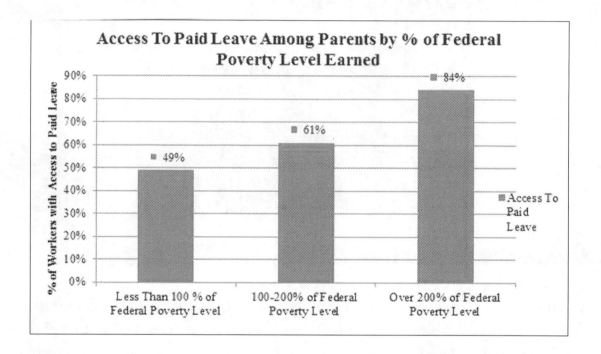

It would certainly be a better world if every person who was responsible for a child had the economic and social support needed to raise them. But the fact is that many of the working poor lack that support.

If you are honest about it, you know that you may have some very strong opinions and feelings about how in the world some people get into the parenting situations they find themselves in. But regardless of that, their children are there, and the immediate needs of these children often impact your business directly.

But it is also important to remember that these child care-related problems only arise because the parents are trying to work, to hold down a responsible job, and to care for and support their children. The difficulties for these working parents are already high. Even minimal support from their workplace can make a world of difference in their lives, and in the lives of their children.

WHY IT COUNTS

"Look Peggy, I'm sorry James called in, but he did. He said his daughter was sick and he had to keep her home from school. She's only seven, and you know since his wife passed away, he's the only one taking care of her." said Jamal Jackson, the lighting department supervisor at the Build-A-Lot hardware and building supply store. "That's why I need you to work an extra three hours today. We need to get the new lighting display up before tomorrow."

"I would Jamal," replied Peggy, "but I have to pick Lara up at the day care before they close at 6:00 this evening. If I don't they'll charge me $60.00 an hour for every hour I'm late in picking her up. I don't have the money to pay that much even if I wanted to."

Peggy was also a single parent; whose two year old Lara was in a local day care. Peggy dropped Lara at the day care when she came to work; then picked her up after work.

Today, because James had called in, Jamal was really short-handed. It was frustrating to him because this wasn't the first time his schedule had been affected by his worker's child care problems!

1. Assume you were James; would you have gone to work or called in? _____

2. Assume you were Peggy; would you stay at work? _____

3. What would you advise Jamal to do if Peggy leaves to pick up her daughter?

   _____

   _____

What To Do

Review the suggested low-cost activities below to determine if your own employees would benefit from them. If so, identify a target date for their implementation, then follow up to document your completion of the activity.

Suggested Management Activity	**Target Date**	**Completion Date**
• Investigate the possibility of forming baby-sitting co-ops consisting of working parents within your own organization. Use of the co-op services only for job-related needs can be built into the system and with some organizational assistance from management could readily become a valuable asset to parents and their employers.	____/____	____/____
• Many lower paid workers need help when attempting to collect child support payments legally due to them. If appropriate, consider investigating the court system in your community to help single parents navigate the procedures		

that are in place to assist when child
support payments are not being made to
single parents caring for their minor-aged
children. Make the acquired information
or contact person identified known to
applicable workers.   ____/____   ____/____

- Be "family friendly" by also being
"worker friendly." Rather than employ
exclusively "family-friendly" policies that
may be viewed as unfair by some, review
scheduling, attendance and leave policies
to ensure they are "employee-friendly,"
thus ensuring perks or benefits are offered
to all employees who qualify, regardless of
parental status.   ____/____   ____/____

- For example, if parent-friendly flex-time
is made available to parents, it can be
made available to all employees. Thus, if
a parent is allowed to arrive 15 minutes
late due to dropping a child off at daycare,
then employees without children would not
be penalized for arriving 15 minutes late
because of a non-child-related emergency
or issue.   ____/____   ____/____

- To help promote work group cohesiveness
take the time to carefully explain your
own family-friendly work policies to those
without children. These workers could

harbor feelings of resentment if they
feel they have been pressured to work
extra shifts or week-ends that working
parents may not be able to work. Assure
these workers that you understand
accommodating working parents cannot
be allowed to unfairly discriminate against
childless employees.   ____/____   ____/____

- On a twice-yearly basis, assess all
promotion and employee evaluation
programs to ensure these do not unfairly
penalize working parents whose on-the-job
performance is excellent but who may not
have the flexibility to work unexpected
longer hours or specific days of the week
due to their childcare responsibilities.   ____/____   ____/____

WHY IT WORKS

✓ **For Your Employees**
It takes a community to raise a child. But what do you do when you don't have anyone but you? What do you do when you're poor? With little money and with little assistance from a support group, many working poor parents have difficulty being excellent parents, even with the best of intentions. Your aid can give these parents the encouragement they need to keep going; and to help them achieve their dreams and the dreams they have for their children.

✓ **For You and Your Organization**

When you show parents that you truly care about the welfare of their children you immediately gain an incredible amount of respect, admiration and gratitude from those parents. The result is a level of employee loyalty that you have truly earned, not mandated. The difference is profound.

Take It Away

"I have always believed helping your fellow man is profitable in every sense, personally and bottom line."

Mario Puzo

Concerning Diversity

What You Know

Diversity at work is usually viewed as a good thing by management, but diversity can easily cause workers to be treated unfairly.

Race is the first issue that usually comes to mind when diversity is considered, but there are many other factors that are equal in separating people and causing unnecessary work place tension.

Diversity simply means variety. Who are these diverse people in your work force? They are simply those who are considered by others to be <u>different</u> from the norm. Differences come in many forms including:

- ✓ Gender
- ✓ Age
- ✓ Physical attractiveness
- ✓ Sexual orientation

- ✓ Tattoos
- ✓ Body piercings
- ✓ Weight
- ✓ Height
- ✓ Dress
- ✓ Religious belief
- ✓ Physical conditions including:
    - challenges related to general health
    - challenges related to hearing
    - challenges related to speech
- ✓ Movement limitations (for example, those with walkers or in wheelchairs)
- ✓ Visible physical differences including missing fingers, hands, arms or legs
- ✓ Differences in mental capacity
- ✓ Differences in social setting interactions (for example those exhibiting extreme shyness, attention deficiencies, phobias or hyper activity)

Some differences are the result of an individual's personal choices; others are not.

Either way, they rarely tell us much about the real character of a person. In most cases, there is very little connection between visible differences that create diversity and those true differences that exist in each person's heart.

For example, you know that strength of character, positive attitude, drive, endurance, loyalty, and compassion can exist in diverse workers of any type. The real differences between good workers and less valuable workers are not based on what they look like; but on whom they really are.

In most cases, visual differences merely demonstrate a person's individualism or show the specific physical challenges they face every day. Rarely do they tell us very much about their true character.

Diversity does reveal something else however. The way in which a person reacts to the visible differences of others illuminates the true nature of their own character.

WHY IT COUNTS

"I just don't think he would be accepted by the crews," said Lawson.

"But you agree he is the most qualified. Right?" replied Sue Kline.

Lawson and Sue were both managers at Deluxe Cinema. The Deluxe Cinema complex consisted of 15 individual showing rooms and two large IMAX theaters. The 17-theater complex employed a large number of ticket takers, concession workers, cleaners and film operators. Most were part time and lower-waged workers.

Lawson managed the day shift, and Sue the evening shift. The theater also employed four hourly paid supervisors who worked 24-32 hours per week and were assigned to different day and evening shifts based on how busy the theater was expected to be.

They were discussing George Firth. George had been with the theater for two years and had proven himself to be a dedicated and talented employee. Sue was recommending he be promoted to fill the newest supervisor vacancy, working on both her and Lawson's shifts.

But George stuttered, sometimes quite badly.

"Yes, he's qualified . . . but you know . . . the stuttering can be a problem. You've heard the joking and teasing that goes on around here about him when he isn't around. You can't stop it," replied Lawson.

"So you don't think we should give him a chance to prove himself?" said Sue.

1. Do you think George has already had to overcome challenges to demonstrate how good he is in his current job? _____

2. How do you think the business would be affected if George was given the supervisor's job? _____

3. How do you think other hourly workers with their own challenges would be affected if they saw George promoted to the Supervisor's position?

_____

What To Do

Review the suggested low-cost activities below to determine if your own employees would benefit from them. If so, identify a target date for their implementation, then follow up to document your completion of the activity.

Suggested Management Activity	Target Date	Completion Date
Develop and implement a "Zero Tolerance" policy toward discrimination and harassment based on worker characteristics that define the diverse nature of your work force. Review the policy in a regular basis.	____/____	____/____
Be aware of your employees' history, life experiences, and character. Take one half hour each week to meet with hourly workers one-on-one or in a group to familiarize yourself with who they are, rather than who they appear to be.	____/____	____/____

- Make sure your work environment is worker-friendly for employees who may possess physical, mental or social limitations. Stay current with changing recommendations and best practices regarding the Americans With Disabilities Act (ADA) at www.ada.gov.   ____/____   ____/____

- Honor your diverse employees by consistently removing from your work force those supervisors or hourly employees who would belittle or undermine the efforts of workers who face and overcome challenges resulting from the nature of their own diversity characteristics.   ____/____   ____/____

- Arrange once per month work place opportunities such as lunch breaks, coffee breaks, snack breaks or other social settings that bring those from diverse backgrounds together to get to know each other on a personal level. Ensure the event encourages personal interaction among diverse employees and their supervisors.   ____/____   ____/____

WHY IT WORKS

✓ **For Your Employees**
Regardless of the source of diversity, employees who are different deal with many issues. Physical struggles, mental struggles, and emotional struggles are

often unavoidable for many. The work place doesn't need to produce more. Work is better for everyone when we stop finding fault with each other for differences that really don't matter, and instead begin valuing each other's true self.

✓ **For You and Your Organization**

Many wonderful individuals have lost opportunities and been dismissed over diversity issues that created barriers to their success. Others who simply "looked good" have gone on to create innumerable work-related problems because it took so long for others to see their true character; because it was so well hidden under their highly presentable exteriors. If you can learn to overlook visible differences that truly don't matter, you better your chances of surrounding yourself with the best employees; the ones who maximize your organization's chance for success.

Take It Away

"When you judge another you do not define them; you define yourself."

Wayne Dyer

SECTION 3

Assisting With Training and Education

Committing to On-the-Job Training

What You Know

A commitment to the value of training workers requires a deep rethinking of your role as a leader and an honest assessment of your workplace. When that happens, you quickly recognize that, as a learning leader, you are the person most responsible for helping your employees develop the skills and attitudes needed to do their jobs well.

In business, assessing a commitment to training is sometimes a bit like assessing "Mom" and "Apple Pie". Everyone, in theory, is in favor. But to be truly committed to the value of training all supervisors and managers must thoughtfully address four key issues:

1. Why should I offer training to my workers?

Ultimately, the only valid reason for providing a training program is because you believe it will equip your workers with the tools they need to perform better in their jobs. Unless your worker productivity is currently at 100%, the answer to this question is obvious.

2. What will happen if I don't train my workers?

Let's face it; most business leaders are optimists. We tend to think things will always work out for the best. But in the area of employee training, we must be realistic. If we know that a lack of commitment to training will put us at a competitive disadvantage or leave a current productivity problem unresolved, then we have an obligation to our own boss, and to ourselves, to implement effective training programs.

3. Will training programs be worth their cost?

Experienced managers know that deferring training costs is like deferring the payment of taxes. In both cases, the costs are real. You can avoid paying them in the short run, but if you wait, they must still be paid, and with a penalty for late payment! They also know that, in nearly all cases, training doesn't cost; it pays.

4. What are my alternatives?

A commitment to training is a bit like a commitment to exercising. Both take time and effort, and in both cases, the alternatives are worse! The alternative to training workers is to rely on the "hope" that your workers will do what must be done without being taught exactly how to do it. "Hope" may be an effective strategy to use when you are at a casino or buying a lottery ticket, but as a business strategy, . . . well let's just say your boss, and your workers are counting on you to do better!

WHY IT COUNTS

"Twenty Bucks? He actually said twenty bucks? That's it? I can't believe that," said Pauline shaking her head.

"Believe it. Twenty bucks, . . . I heard him," said Stan.

Pauline was the general manager and Stan was the supervising cashier at Water World Family Water Park. When business was at its seasonal peak, the park employed eight cashiers who were kept busy selling individual and group tickets to the park's customers. Stan supervised the cashiering and sales effort. Stan was relaying to Pauline what he had overheard said Frank, one of the new cashiers, was asked by a guest about the park's new "All-for-One" family package.

"Tell me again what happened," said Pauline.

"O.K., a man came to the counter to claim the four individual tickets he had reserved online. Four tickets at $29.75, for a total of $119. Then the guest saw one of our new "All-for-One" posters advertising the new $139 family package," said Stan.

"Right, that's exactly why we had the posters made up," said Pauline. "It's good for us because it builds our revenue per guest. And with free drink refills, $5.00 off each pizza purchase and two for one ice cream, it's a real money saver for families. So what happened next?"

Well, then this guest looks at the poster again and he asks Stan, "What's the difference between the four individual tickets for $119 and the $139 package . . . . and that's when Randy said it," said Stan.

"Twenty bucks," said Pauline.

"Twenty bucks," replied Stan.

1. Why do you think Randy answered "Twenty Bucks" to this guest's question? _____

2. Who was hurt most by his response? _____
    _____

3. Who do you think is responsible for the quality of Randy's responses to similar guest queries? _____ _____

4. What do you think will happen in the future if Pauline and Stan <u>do not</u> commit to an effective training program for their workers in positions similar to Randy's? _____
    _____

What To Do

Review the suggested low-cost activities below to determine if your own employees would benefit from them. If so, identify a target date for their implementation, then follow up to document your completion of the activity.

Suggested Management Activity	Target Date	Completion Date
• Develop a brief written statement that summarizes your personal commitment to providing training for all your new employees. Review this formal statement during new employee orientation while explaining its implications for each new worker's future within your organization.	____/____	____/____

- Develop a new employee mentor program that pairs a well-trained employee with each newly hired worker.   ____/____   ____/____

- Review and document, in their personal file, the unique learning abilities and limitations of each newly hired employee. Note especially each employee's reading, hearing and language abilities. Refer to these documents when developing targeted training activities.   ____/____   ____/____

- Recognize that attitude training is just as important as skills training in most lower-waged positions. Develop and implement one training activity per year that emphasizes the importance of a positive attitude for achieving job success in your organization.   ____/____   ____/____

- Identify cross-training opportunities for as many of your lower-waged workers as is reasonably possible. Cross-training demonstrates to workers that you have faith in their abilities and want to provide them with opportunities for career growth.   ____/____   ____/____

WHY IT WORKS

✓ **For Your Employees**
People have more confidence and feel more empowered when they know exactly what is expected of them. Jobs actually become easier and more enjoyable for employees who understand what is required of them. Their own self-image will improve when they are supplied with the tools and knowledge needed to accomplish their work assignments.

✓ **For You and Your Organization**
You pay your employees to come to the jobsite to do the work you need done. It only makes sense then for you to ensure that they are doing exactly what you want done, and that the work is done in the most cost effective way possible. You reduce costs and eliminate confusion when you commit to training all of your staff members effectively.

Take It Away

> *"What if we train our people and they leave? . . .*
> *But what if we <u>don't</u> train them and they stay?"*
>
> *Unknown*

Implementing On-the-Job Training and Education

What You Know

You have no doubt witnessed the magical moments that occur when a baby initially learns how to walk.

As those first tentative steps are taken the baby is delighted; but perhaps not nearly as much as the parents or relatives who hold out their hands, verbally express their encouragement and excitedly reward even the tiniest of steps.

Babies will learn to walk naturally, of course, but no one can deny the value of the enthusiastic support so freely given to them as they learn to do it successfully.

Learning is the basis for success and forward progress in all human endeavors. Whether acquired through formal education within an educational institution or by hands-on experiences at work, people who learn, and then apply their knowledge can simply go farther, and are more successful, than those who don't.

In our society, many lower-waged workers may have had limited opportunities to train or educate themselves. Their positions and income level may have afforded them little time and few resources for personal growth.

That does not mean, however, that they don't desire or appreciate the benefits afforded by learning and training. As a leader, you have the unique opportunity to help them learn the skills necessary to radically improve their confidence as a worker, as a higher functioning individual, and as a valuable part of your organization.

But that can only happen when you take the time to encourage their development and when you share their pride in accomplishing what you know they can do; if only they get the encouragement they need to take their first steps toward success.

WHY IT COUNTS

"I can't do it," said Latoya looking up at Phyllis in frustration . . . "It's too hard, and I'm just not coordinated enough."

The line of customers was backing up at the deli/meat counter at Ben's market and Phyllis, the store's manager, could see why.

Ben's Market was widely known in the area as a high quality retail purveyor of fine foods, wine and cheeses. The deli/ meat counter was a particularly popular spot with customers as the market stocked USDA primes cuts of beef, many imported cured meats and sausages, and a wide variety of organic chicken, pork and turkey products.

While product quality was excellent at Ben's, Phyllis knew the real reason for the market's success was the high level of service provided to customers in the produce, dairy, grocery and deli/meat departments.

But today, service at the deli/ meat counter was slow, very slow.

It was Latoya's second day working the counter. While Latoya had been with the market for six months, and had an outstanding attitude and attendance record, it appeared now that moving Latoya from her previous job pre-packing meats to a front line guest service position may have been a mistake.

Whole organic chickens were on sale, and many of the market's customers wanted to choose their bird from the refrigerated display case, and have their selection freshly cut for them. That meant cutting the chickens into 8 pieces, a somewhat tricky process that required the cuts to be made precisely and neatly to avoid damaging the look of the poultry. To keep the lines moving, and to serve the market's customers in a prompt manner, it also needed to be done quickly.

Latoya was not doing it precisely, neatly, or quickly. It was clear she had not had enough practice to do the 8-cut properly. When she noticed the customer back up Phyllis had approached Latoya, and that's when Latoya had looked up at her from the cutting table.

1. What message will Phyllis send if she decides to return Latoya to a non-customer service role in the meat/ deli department? _____

_____

2. What message will Phyllis send if she "finds" the hour or so needed to provide the specific skills training Latoya needs to master the task of 8-cutting the chicken? _____

_____

3. Which decision do you think would be best for the long-term interests of:
    i.   Latoya? _____
    ii. Phyllis? _____
    iii. The customers at Ben's? _____
    iv. Other hourly-paid workers at Ben's? _____

What To Do

Review the suggested low-cost activities below to determine if your own employees would benefit from them. If so, identify a target date for their implementation, then follow up to document your completion of the activity.

Suggested Management Activity	**Target Date**	**Completion Date**
• Consider each of the jobs you supervise in your organization. Identify the five key skills needed for success in each of them. Then determine the training plan you must implement to ensure all five key skills are acquired by all of your workers.	____/____	____/____
• Busy managers can rarely "find" the time to train. Instead, they must "make" the time. Evaluate your own work schedule. "Find" one hour per week which you can commit		

to the training needs of your lower-waged
employees. Pledge to yourself that you will
use that one hour each week to address
those critical needs. Over time the results
will be immense.   ____/____   ____/____

- There are a tremendous number of training
  aids available to managers who are
  committed to providing quality training.
  Google "Employee Training Tools" and
  choose a web site that provides no-cost
  or low-cost training tips you can apply
  immediately in your own organization.   ____/____   ____/____

- The evaluation of training efforts is just
  as important as training delivery. Identify
  effective ways to determine if the training
  you delivered really "worked". Ask employees
  for their opinion and measure actual
  post-training results. Continually revise and
  modify your delivery of on-the-job training
  programs to improve their effectiveness.   ____/____   ____/____

- Celebrate your workers' successes.
  Inexpensive gifts, certificates and plaques
  are an excellent way to publicly recognize
  those employees who have successfully
  completed required training. The impact
  of these rewards is especially significant to
  lower-waged workers whose educational
  successes may have been limited in the past.   ____/____   ____/____

WHY IT WORKS

✓ **For Your Employees**

Knowledge, experience, and training are essential parts of life. Not only on the job but throughout everything we do in our lives. By giving employees the benefits that come from increasing their skills and knowledge, and subsequently giving them the confidence that comes from a job well done, you will empower many of them to become more than they ever imagined they could be.

✓ **For You and Your Organization**

Taking the time to train and education your employees will inevitably build a stronger, more effective and more efficient work force. You will spend less time putting out fires; and that will allow you to do what you do best: manage, innovate . . . and build your business.

Take It Away

> *"Tell me and I'll forget.*
> *Show me and I may remember.*
> *Involve me and I'll understand."*
>
> *Chinese Proverb*

Creating Career Ladders

What You Know

Some jobs have easily identifiable career paths. In your own job, you may be able to readily see where you could be in five, ten or twenty years. Not all jobs are like that, however.

For some lower-waged workers, seeing advancement in their own futures is not so easy. Does that mean that no destination exists for them? Of course not.

Even though it may not be easy to see, and there is no universal goal for every person, there is a journey for each of us to take. These destinations can differ greatly; but the important thing to remember is that everyone needs one of their own.

Considering career advancement is similar to planning an exciting vacation. Desire is natural. Even though the trip is not usually immediate, the anticipation begins as soon as you know you might go. The planning, the goals, the preparations become an enjoyable part of the journey because of the expectation of the reward. The best dreams are just outside our reach, yet reasonable enough to believe we can actually do it. It doesn't work to envision something outside the realm of possibility. People face real-life limitations.

First; where will you go and is it realistic to assume you can get there?

Do you have the financial resources to fly? Or drive? Or walk?

Is time a factor?

In general, do you have what you need to go places others may not? Or do you have restrictions that limit your choices?

If you think about it, it's easy to see that each individual's personal situation will influence their ability to determine and then reach their ideal destination. Some will experience the world's greatest wonders. Others may realistically need to settle for enjoying the sights and sounds of their local city parks. That's reality. There is, however, beauty everywhere if you look for it. The important thing to remember is that everyone should be allowed to anticipate a new destination and enjoy the excitement that accompanies that journey.

Job progress doesn't simply happen. It must be planned for. And you are the ideal person to help each of your workers plan their personal job journey.

WHY IT COUNTS

"She said she felt like she wasn't getting anywhere Gabe," said Sandy. "She said she needed a change."

"But that doesn't make any sense," said Gabe Thompson, Sandy's co-supervisor.

Sandy and Gabe were talking about Carol, one of their best and longest term hourly employees.

At the end of her shift yesterday Carol had asked if she could speak to Sandy alone. When they entered Sandy's office, Carol had announced she had accepted another job, and would be starting it in two weeks.

Generally, when an hourly employee announced they were leaving to take a job with a competitor, they were let go on the spot. But Sandy liked Carol, and would miss her ability and upbeat attitude. So she had taken the extra time to try and find out what was really going on.

"I know," replied Sandy, "Carol said the money was the same, and she'd start with them doing the same work she does here. She said it was the chance to move up that sold her on the change."

1. Do you think it will be an organization's most talented workers, or it's least talented, that would leave in search of career advancement? _____
   _____

2. Assuming they are in the same business segment, do you think Carol's new employer will be offering her anything in the way of career progression that Sandy and Lionel could not have offered? _____
   Why do you think her current supervisors did not offer Carol the opportunity to advance? _____

3. Have you ever lost a good hourly employee to a competitor you knew offered no greater career opportunities to that employee than your own organization? _____

What To Do

Review the suggested low-cost activities below to determine if your own employees would benefit from them. If so, identify a target date for their implementation, then follow up to document your completion of the activity.

Suggested Management Activity	Target Date	Completion Date
• Meet with each of your hourly employees to see where they feel their own skills and abilities can take them in your organization.	____/____	____/____
• Take the time to personally assess each of your hourly employees' career limits. Don't set their final destination further than they are willing or able to go, but commit to taking them further than they are today, and then communicate your vision to them.	____/____	____/____
• Be creative with the destinations your employees can strive to reach. For some it may only involve meeting punctuality or attendance goals. In all cases, plan the actions you must take to help them set and reach their new goals.	____/____	____/____
• Consider establishing "steps" or "levels" for hourly employees. For example, a Level 1, Level 2 and Level 3 job classification. Establish standards for reaching these		

higher levels within a job and communicate
those standards to all affected hourly
employees.   ____/____   ____/____

- Celebrate employee achievement. Publicly
  recognize the progress of hourly employees
  when they move up the steps of the career
  ladders you have established for them.   ____/____   ____/____

WHY IT WORKS

✓ **For Your Employees**

All workers want to feel they are successful. One important component of
success involves setting goals and then achieving them. For many workers,
advancement potential in their jobs may be limited; for others it may not.
In either case, the career ladder you establish for your lower-waged workers
should be a step ladder. And every person in your organization should have the
opportunity, and the real hope, of climbing a rung or two!

✓ **For You and Your Organization**

As an effective manager, part of the reason for your success is undoubtedly
your ability to set goals and achieve them. That's probably a big part of why
you are where you are today. But if you look back, someone surely helped you
get where you are. They pointed the way for you. Because that's true, you know
how to help others take their own steps forward, and as they move ahead so will
your business.

Take It Away

*"Success in life means having the courage, the will,
<u>and</u> the opportunity;
to become the persons we were meant to be."*

George Sheehan

Aiding in Off-Site Educational Opportunities

What You Know

You know that not every rock is a diamond. Miners have to sort through a lot of rocks hoping to get lucky and find just one diamond. And even when they do, a diamond doesn't come out of the ground all shiny, bright and beautifully cut.

In fact, creating a diamond from a rough stone is a three-step process. Most people know about Step Two (the cutting) and Step Three (the polishing). But those in the diamond business know that "Splitting", Step One in the process, is actually the most critical.

When creating a diamond, the "Splitter" first examines the rough stone very carefully and then decides how it should be shaped to retain the utmost weight with the most brilliant effect. The Splitter carefully assesses every flaw and streak, and he or she must determine whether the observed imperfections are at the stone's surface or at its heart. It takes all of a Splitter's insight, knowledge and experience to transform an uncut diamond into a thing of beauty.

In many ways, some of the lower-waged workers who walk in your door resemble uncut diamonds. They arrive without every facet of their potential skills and knowledge perfected. As a manager it is part of your job to find, assess, and help to refine those workers who have the desire and capability to become the diamonds in your workplace.

What you will find as you identify the best of your best is that not everything they need to know can be taught through their daily work experience. Language skills, computer literacy, math, reading, writing, finances, and many other crucial employee skills are, however, taught through local community programs, adult learning centers, and community colleges, as well as through online courses. Many of these are free or very low cost and completing them can really help your employees polish skills that will make them more valuable to you and your business.

A diamond doesn't find itself. It takes a person to search for it and recognize its potential. Once you've done, that the final polishing is pretty easy.

WHY IT COUNTS

"Look," said Emily, "you're not listening to me. I'm Sylvia's biggest fan."

"Then why are you opposed to moving her up?" asked Franklin.

Emily and Franklin were discussing Sylvia Zepeda. Sylvia had started in their hotel as an hourly housekeeper four years earlier. While not a native English speaker, during the time she had been with the hotel she had learned the language quickly and had improved her spoken English dramatically.

She was also a dedicated worker, with perfect attendance, excellent guest service skills and tremendous attention to detail.

For all of those reasons, Franklin, the hotel's Rooms Manager was recommending Sylvia be promoted to a mid-level management position that meant more responsibility and more money for Sylvia.

"It's the written reports," said Emily. "You know that the new job would mean she needs to write up the weeklies and the monthlies. It's hard enough to write those reports when you can speak and write English easily. Promoting her would be like asking you to write a report in Spanish. Could you do that?" asked Emily.

"But other than that she's perfect for the job, "said Franklin, "and besides, think about the positive message we would be sending the other room attendants if we moved her up."

1. Why do you think Emily feels moving Sylvia up would be a bad idea?

   _____

2. Do you think the type of skills training needed to help Sylvia move up is likely available in her local community _____
   Based on what you know about her, do you think Sylvia likely has the ability to master the skills she would need to advance in the hotel? _____

3. Whose responsibility is it to prepare Sylvia to move up in this business?

   _____

   Whose responsibility is it to help her? _____

What To Do

Review the suggested low-cost activities below to determine if your own employees would benefit from them. If so, identify a target date for their implementation, then follow up to document your completion of the activity.

Suggested Management Activity	Target Date	Completion Date
• Contact your local school district to obtain a listing of low-cost or no-cost educational programs offered to adult learners in your community. Evaluate the list for courses that can help your hourly employees do their current jobs better as well as jobs that may be in their future. Communicate your findings to employees who could benefit from the course offerings.	____/____	____/____
• Surf the web to identify any available online training courses that can directly benefit your employees. Trade associations, local schools, and community colleges are potential sources of online coursework.	____/____	____/____

• Many hourly employees may lack high speed internet access in their homes. Consider the possibility of developing an on-site "training room" with high speed internet access that can be made available

to hourly employees for the completion of
their "off-site" educational programs.

____/____   ____/____

- Consider establishing modest tuition grants
  to reward those employees who successfully
  complete off-site course work that directly
  benefits your organization.

____/____   ____/____

- Be as flexible as possible in scheduling
  workers around off-site courses they are
  attending. Communicate to employees that
  the scheduling flexibility is a reward you
  are glad to provide to demonstrate your
  commitment to their efforts.

____/____   ____/____

- Remind your employees that success in life
  is best measured not by where you are; but
  by how far you have come.

____/____   ____/____

WHY IT WORKS

✓ **For Your Employees**
Potential is a horrible thing to waste. There is no doubt that some of your
employees desire more for themselves and for their families. And some of them
have abilities that are untapped. It's often the case they have never been given
the opportunities and encouragement necessary to grow. Everyone deserves a
chance.

✓ **For You and Your Organization**

A great business staff doesn't just appear. You have to develop it. That takes effort on your part, as well as your employees; but it's most often worth that effort; because diamonds help you outshine your competitors.

Take It Away

> *"Education is for improving the lives of others;*
> *and for leaving your community and world better than you found it."*
>
> *Marian Wright Edelman*

SECTION 4

Improving Workers' Health

Recognizing the Impact of Health on Productivity

What You Know

The old adage, "An apple a day keeps the doctor away" isn't just a statement on the nutritional value of an apple. You know that the implications are much bigger than that.

Being pro-active in regards to healthy living and healthy eating, along with other health factors, will result in less illness and subsequently fewer health-related problems. And everyone knows that employees' health-related issues cost their employers big time. How big?

The U.S. Department of Labor statistics estimates that the overall impact of negative health issues on America's 137 million workers exceeds 1.7 trillion dollars per year.

Most employers know that worker absenteeism costs them in lost productivity, diminished customer service levels, and the over-burdening of those workers who did not call in sick.

What fewer employers recognize is that "presenteeism" is just as big a problem. Presenteeism is simply what happens when workers should stay home sick; but elect to come to work anyway because they fear losing income or their jobs.

Presentee workers are less productive, make more mistakes, and can even make their co-workers sick. According to a recent Duke University study, one of eight lower-waged workers surveyed said they had come to work at least twice in the previous 12 months while suffering from diarrhea or vomiting. That's 12% of all lower-waged workers!

It's easy to see that the fewer sick days missed or (sick days worked!) by your employees, the better off they and your organization will be.

You may not be in a position to offer paid time off to your lower-waged employees, but you can take positive steps to create a more healthful work environment that will pay big dividends for them and for you. Some of these steps include addressing these low-cost but important health-related areas that can make the workplace more pleasurable!

⇒ Stress: Minimize it wherever possible.
⇒ Laughter: Encourage it because having fun increases health.
⇒ Movement: Build it into sedentary jobs
⇒ Fresh air and sunlight: Make the workplace as natural as possible.

WHY IT COUNTS

"Cover for me Hank," said Lee, "I'll be right back."

"Hey man, there must be 30 people in the line. What's going on?" replied Hank.

"I just gotta go, . . . I'll be right back" said Lee as he walked quickly to the employee restroom area.

Hank and Lee were the parking attendants for the valet lot servicing the Grand Theater. The Grand was the largest special events auditorium in the area. City-owned, the Grand had its own parking area two blocks away, but many event attendees elected the convenience of valet parking in the lot directly adjacent to the theater. That lot was operated by Richard's Valet Parking Services; the company that employed Hank and Lee.

It was about 10:00 p.m. and the Grand's Saturday night Broadway-style presentation of "Mama Mia" was just letting out.

Lee had taken about four short breaks since he had arrived at work and Hank had noticed when he had come in that Lee didn't look so good.

The immediate problem was that the theater attendees who had valet parked their cars were now lined up to retrieve them. Hank and Lee were the only two parking lot attendants on duty and Hank knew that theater goers who chose to valet park their cars were usually pretty impatient to get them when the show was over.

Now, with Lee gone again, the customers' wait times would be longer, and the people waiting in line would grow even more impatient. And that also meant his tips would be lower.

1. Why do you think Lee is taking so many breaks? _____
2. Why do think Lee elected to come to work? _____
3. Do you think the theater goers who waited in line this night will be more or less likely to choose Richard's Valet Parking Services the next time they attend an event at the Grand? _____

What To Do

Review the suggested low-cost activities below to determine if your own employees would benefit from them. If so, identify a target date for their implementation, then follow up to document your completion of the activity.

Suggested Management Activity	**Target Date**	**Completion Date**
• Invest in a speaker or intercom system to provide background music in work areas. Allow workers the maximum allowable input on the types of music to be played.	____/____	____/____
• Carefully evaluate the lighting levels in all work areas, as well as break areas. Ensure lighting levels help to create an inviting work atmosphere.	____/____	____/____
• Carefully evaluate the air quality in all work areas, as well as break. Ensuring adequate fresh air helps create a productive and healthy work atmosphere.	____/____	____/____

- Consider allowing time for employees to communicate with sick family and friends (within set limits). The ability to stay in touch with sick-at-home children or parents can significantly reduce stress levels of primary caregivers and pay big dividends in worker loyalty.

  ____/____   ____/____

- Dehydration is one of the workplace's most misunderstood threats to worker health. Encouraging employees to drink cool water frequently (ideally at 60-65 ° F and that you provide free to them) and in small volume rather than hot tea, coffee or carbonated drinks to compensate for losses due to sweating or high work place temperatures.

  ____/____   ____/____

- Make nutritional snacks (and maybe even nutritional lunches or dinners!) available to your employees at a cost both you and they can afford.

  ____/____   ____/____

- Review your work area to identify an adequate space for employee rest areas and stretch/workout areas. Encourage employees to use these areas before and after work; or during their meal breaks.

  ____/____   ____/____

- Double the number of your workers' paid breaks. Yes, you read that right! Productivity studies consistently show

that the total amount of work that will
be completed will actually increase
(not decrease!); and worker health and
satisfaction will increase as well.   ____/____   ____/____

WHY IT WORKS

✓ **For Your Employees**
Some work in lower-waged jobs can be fairly tedious, monotonous, and stressful.
Small things can make the day much more enjoyable and aid worker's good
health. Fresh air, nutritious snacks, adequate breaks and the chance to stretch
or exercise can all help to decrease the amount of mental and physical stress
your employees endure though out the work day. And healthier employees
come to work more often.

✓ **For You and Your Organization**
Healthy employees are more productive, more cooperative, and less prone to
absenteeism. Keeping your work force healthy and efficient are two primary
concerns as a manager. Reducing employee sick days also means less stress
in your own job. Being pro-active in the area of worker health has consistently
shown itself to be a win-win situation for workers and for managers.

Take It Away

> *"Pleasure in the job puts perfection in the work."*
>
> *Aristotle*

Ensuring Safety on the Job

What You Know

In this day and age of law suits, you can't protect yourself enough from the problems arising from safety mishaps. But as important as that is, there is another reason to be ever aware of the safety of your employees; "Common Sense".

No business can operate effectively when it workers' safety and security are under constant threat. The "3 Stooges" always made us laugh from their slips, blunders, eye pokes, and head bumps. In reality there is nothing funny about any of these things at work.

Workplace injuries and illnesses constitute a major concern both for lower-waged workers and their families. That's because a work-related injury or illness takes a secondary toll on those who depend on your workers. If they cannot work due to an injury or illness, what will the family do for money? How will they financially survive the crisis?

It's no big surprise that employees cannot do their jobs or function properly in the constant presence of danger or the fear of what will happen to those they love if they do get hurt. And they certainly cannot perform their job up to standards when suffering from work-related injuries.

And it's also no big surprise that the costs of work-place injury are high. These include:

- ✓ Productive time lost by an injured employee
- ✓ Productive time lost by employees and supervisors attending to the accident victim
- ✓ Clean up of the job site or process interrupted by the accident
- ✓ Time to hire or to retrain other individuals to replace the injured worker until his/her return
- ✓ Time and cost for repair or replacement of any damaged equipment or products
- ✓ Cost of potential workers' compensation claims and increased workers' compensation insurance rates
- ✓ Reduced morale among remaining non-injured employees
- ✓ Time expended to complete reports or paperwork caused by the incident

The lost revenue and lost productivity that occurs when an employee is injured is unrecoverable. With determined awareness and reasonable precautions, however, you can go a long way toward minimizing the chance of employee injury and maximizing the healthfulness of your work site.

WHY IT COUNTS

"That's exactly why we need to change," said Karis, the production supervisor at Cason Industries.

Karis was talking with Carlos, her plant manager, about her new hourly employees' performance on the safety training modules all Cason Industries workers were required to complete.

The fact was that safety-related injuries had been increasing in the plant, and especially among the plant's younger workers.

Carlos had been discussing with Karis his frustration with the inability of the plant's younger workers to absorb the material in the safety-training manuals and workbooks that had been so carefully prepared for them.

"Look Carlos," said Karis, "Unfortunately, brochures and handbooks do not work as well as they used to. Computer-based modules and social marketing tools are more effective ways to improve safety in the workplace today. That's what I've been saying".

"So you want to create YouTube training?" asked Carlos shaking his head.

"What I'm telling you," replied Karis, "is that they aren't getting it. That's a fact. In today's culture, media is an extremely important part of effective communication, especially between young people. We have to communicate with them on their level, not ours. That is, . . . if we want to keep the plant's accident-related costs down. I say we use the tools they are familiar with. And yes; . . . that includes YouTube!"

1. How important do you think it is to communicate critical information such as safe work practices in a way that is highly appealing to diverse workers?

    _____

2. What do you think will happen to the safety record of younger workers at this plant if no change is made in how they are taught worker safety?

    _____

3. What do you think will happen to injury-related costs at this plant if no change is made in how younger workers are taught safety information?

_____

What To Do

Review the suggested low-cost activities below to determine if your own employees would benefit from them. If so, identify a target date for their implementation, then follow up to document your completion of the activity.

Suggested Management Activity	Target Date	Completion Date
• Have safety precautions printed on signage in the language(s) of your employees and displayed in easily viewable locations.	____/____	____/____
• Repair, replace, and maintain the physical safety of your building and surrounding property.	____/____	____/____
• Keep all machinery and equipment properly functioning and checked on a regular basis.	____/____	____/____
• Hold regular safety and security meetings with staff.	____/____	____/____
• Be sure all employees are properly trained in safety techniques and policies.	____/____	____/____

- Keep first aid kits and health and security contact numbers easily accessible and up-to-date.

  ____/____   ____/____

- Implement an inexpensive incentive program to publicly recognize and reward workers for their safe-at-work achievements (i.e. the number of days of accident free work)

  ____/____   ____/____

WHY IT WORKS

✓ **For Your Employees**
No one should be in needless danger of injury while trying to do his or her job. It is not within most employees' power to do the things necessary to totally protect their work environment. It is also not their sole responsibility to understand or recognize potential dangers with chemicals, equipment, and security without proper instructions and training. What's more, lower-waged employees can afford less that most, the medical costs and lost income resulting from on the job injury.

✓ **For You and Your Organization**
Absentee employees, lost productivity, law suits! Need I say more?

Take It Away

*"Planning is bringing the future into the present
so that you can do something about it now."*

Alan Lakein

Addressing Healthy Eating

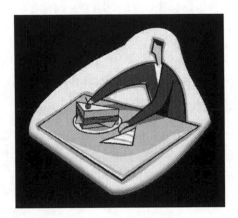

What You Know

In the American culture people are under a lot of stress. Schedules are full, work hours are long, and finances are tight. Instant gratification is part of most people's daily ritual. People want fast, and they want easy. When it comes to food, many also want cheap and they want yummy!

Prepackaged and processed foods would seem to have it all. Large quantities of it have surprisingly low costs. Fried, high-fat, high-salt, and high-sugar foods offer tastes that appeal to our cravings and let us feel pampered. These products are easy to buy, require no cooking time, and are quite affordable. Sounds perfect? Hardly.

With little to no nutritional value they are anything but perfect. And in the U.S. they increasingly are linked to obesity and overall poor health.

There is an additional dilemma. In our culture, eating is tied to socializing, celebrating, breaking boredom and seeking comfort. Since eating is not necessarily associated with hunger, it is easily done to excess.

With all this distraction it is very hard to focus on the true purpose of food consumption. Food is essential to life. It provides fuel for movement, healing, and processing of bodily functions. It isn't possible to change Americans' culture. That isn't the point. Just encouraging one healthy meal during the day and promoting healthy snacking during the workday is vital and can radically change your employee's health and well-being along with productivity and morale.

You wouldn't expect your machinery and vehicles to run properly if you didn't provide fuel or the materials necessary to enable them to run properly. Your employees need the same attention and care.

WHY IT COUNTS

"I gotta sit down for a minute," said Sue.

Margaret could see that Sue was sweating profusely.

Both Sue and Margaret were in their early forties. They worked for the Magic Broom custom home cleaning services. A typical eight-hour workday for them included doing the dusting, vacuuming, washing and sanitizing of five private homes. The company's motto was "No Detail Overlooked."

It was a warm day and Sue and Margaret had just finished bringing all of their cleaning equipment and supplies in from the van they used to go to the homes they had been assigned to clean.

Margaret and Sue had been paired together for about four months. Sue was significantly overweight and while she was strong, it was not unusual for her to take frequent breaks because she got winded easily.

Today the heat and the exertion of lifting the equipment seemed to be affecting her more than usual, and they were already behind schedule.

"O.K', let's take a break," said Margaret reluctantly.

"Good idea," said Sue.

1. What impact do you think Sue's weight issue has on her productivity level for Magic Broom? _____

2. What impact do you think Sue's weight has on Margaret's productivity?

    _____

    On Margaret's morale? _____

3. On a day like this one, how realistic is it to assume Sue will fulfill the company's promise of "No Detail Overlooked"? _____

What To Do

Review the suggested low-cost activities below to determine if your own employees would benefit from them. If so, identify a target date for their implementation, then follow up to document your completion of the activity.

Suggested Management Activity	**Target Date**	**Completion Date**
• Make healthy snacks and healthy beverage options available for employees at reasonable costs.	____/____	____/____
• Encourage healthy choices for lunch through education. Give employees access to refrigerated storage, microwave and a clean, comfortable lunch room.	____/____	____/____
• Help organize group orders for lunch deliveries to reduce costs and improve healthy options.	____/____	____/____
• Organize walk groups during lunch or before/after work.	____/____	____/____
• Encourage healthy eating habits. Make it a policy not to allow employees to skip breaks or lunch in exchange for leaving work early.	____/____	____/____
• Set the standard. Ensure that any foods provided at company sponsored employee outings or picnics are low in fat and sodium and are healthy, fresh and nutritious.	____/____	____/____
• Check out innovative efforts such as Michelle Obama's initiatives to promote healthy eating in the U.S. (www.letsmove.		

<u>gov)</u> to determine if any can be applied in
your workplace.   ____/____   ____/____

WHY IT WORKS

✓ **For Your Employees**
There is a definite link between income, health and weight. For a variety of
reasons, lower income correlates strongly to poor health, lowered physical
activity and weight problems. Obesity is an enormous problem in this country.
Providing healthy food at work is one of the best ways to get people to eat at
least one healthy meal a day. Even one healthy meal a day can shift the balance
toward increasing the heath and happiness of your workers.

✓ **For You and Your Organization**
Paying attention to employees' diet is a step above and beyond what has
previously been perceived as the responsibility of most employers. However the
health of your employees directly impacts your morale, productivity, safety, and
attendance. It's in the best interest of your business, and you, to take whatever
measures are reasonably possible to improve the quality of foods consumed by
employees during their workday and at the workplace.

Take It Away

> *"America's health care system is in crisis*
> *precisely because we systematically neglect wellness and prevention."*
>
> *Tom Harkin*

<u>Accessing Public Assistance Programs</u>

𝐖𝐡𝐚𝐭 𝐘𝐨𝐮 𝐊𝐧𝐨𝐰

Those who are considered to be poor in America have changed dramatically in the post-World War II era. Thanks largely to Social Security and Medicare the poverty rate for the elderly declined from 35.2% in 1959 to 9.7% in 2008.

However, while poverty among seniors is now relatively low, you likely know that the total number of poor is growing and increasingly they are young people. Due in part to the rise of single parent households the poverty rate for children under 6 has risen significantly from a low of 15.3 percent in 1969 (the first year of official data) to well over 21% in 2008.

Not only has the make-up of the poor changed; but the fundamental ways the poor are viewed in America has changed as well. As a result, the last two decades have seen profound changes in U.S. social welfare policies. Implicit in the more conservative approach to social welfare now in place is the popular notion, embraced by most Americans, that able-bodied adult family members, including single parents, should work to support their families and that by working hard these families should be able to escape poverty.

In fact is, the working poor are working more than they ever have! Currently over 38 percent of those in poverty are from families where adult members worked more than half-time jobs. This represents a substantial increase from the 28 percent of persons in poor families with the same number of hours worked in 1982.

The idea that if you work hard enough you can accomplish anything you want rings hollow for many working poor. They are already working hard, and often in more than one job. If hard work alone pulled individuals out of poverty, a large number of minimum wage workers performing back breaking tasks eight hours or more per day would be wealthy. But you know that hard work is not enough. That is the reason our country has established and maintains a multitude of assistance programs to aid those that continue to struggle.

Americans are truly a generous people and as a society are more than willing to share the country's abundance with those truly in need. Many of your employees, however, may simply be unaware of the assistance they are eligible for or don't know how to go about exploring the possibilities. It's most often a simple thing to make this information available to those who need it and qualify for it. Your workers may not know what's available to them, but you can find out, and let them know, and encourage them to get the help available to them.

Listed below are just some of the worker-aid programs found in many states and communities:

- Basic needs supplements
- Health insurance coverage assistance (especially for children)
- Health and dental care
- Housing cost supplements
- Food stamps; food assistance
- Transportation assistance (for home to work)
- Wage supplements
- Earned income tax credits (for those who file their taxes properly)
- Welfare to work supplemental pay (for those who file taxes with the state)
- Assistance with job and career
- Jobs training
- Tuition assistance
- Unemployment insurance
- Temporary unemployment income supplements

WHY IT COUNTS

"Adrian said he didn't call them. He said he's not going. Said he don't want no charity. Said he'd be fine." Lemont Green was reporting a conversation to Mark Larson; his line supervisor at Green-beach Industries, located in Providence Rhode, Island.

"Well, that's just crazy," replied Mark Larson, the manager at Green-beach to whom both Lemont Green and Lemont's co-worker Adrian Washington reported.

It was 7:45 a.m. and Lemont had just delivered to Mark, the message that Adrian would be late because he needed to stop at the drug store and pick up some oil of cloves to put on a sore tooth that had become increasingly painful over the past two days.

Lemont and Mark were discussing Adrian's refusal to call the county dental clinic to deal with what Mark was pretty sure was an infected tooth.

Green-beach did not offer dental insurance to its part-time hourly employees, but Mark's wife worked for the State of Rhode Island's Medical Assistance program, so he knew first hand that the kind of emergency dental treatment Adrian needed was available free of charge to qualifying people. Adrian qualified. And on the previous day, Mark had casually let Adrian know about it.

"Look Lemont, you gotta talk to him again" said Mark, "he qualifies for help. And here in Rhode Island, we have an assistance program just for people like him. It covers root canals. And that's what he needs to get that tooth fixed and be able to get back to work."

"Don't tell me;" replied Lemont, "tell him. But I'm not sure he'll be in much of a position to listen when he gets here. If he gets here."

1. Why do you think some employees like Adrian would be reluctant to ask for, or even receive, services offered by public assistance programs? _____

   _____

2. Assume you were Mark. What would you do now? _____

   _____

3. Assume Adrian works four eight hour shifts per week at Green-beach. What do you think would be the direct impact on business at Green-beach Industries if Adrian missed two of his assigned days of work because of his tooth? _____

   _____

What To Do

Review the suggested low-cost activities below to determine if your own employees would benefit from them. If so, identify a target date for their implementation, then follow up to document your completion of the activity.

	Target Date	Completion Date
Suggested Management Activity		

- Contact the social services department of your state government. Request a list of websites/contact numbers of offices and state agencies that provide aid to qualified employees. Keep the information updated and make it readily available to your staff.   ____/____   ____/____

- Do a web search (Google) to determine if any religious organizations in your area offer general assistance with food, shelter, or transportation needs.   ____/____   ____/____

- Research aid programs that may be made especially available for those working parents who have minor children in their homes.   ____/____   ____/____

- Research aid programs that may be made especially available for those who care for one or more elderly family members in their homes.   ____/____   ____/____

- Contact your State bar association and/ or legal services association to investigate the availability of pro-bono legal services available to resident workers as well as to immigrant employees and their families.   ____/____   ____/____

- Use group meetings to discuss with your employees the aid and support groups you have identified. Encourage them to take advantage of all locally provided aid programs for which they legitimately qualify.   ____/____   ____/____

- Update websites, contact numbers and names of those heading local aid programs at least twice per year.   ____/____   ____/____

WHY IT WORKS

✓ **For Your Employees**
We all have the same number of hours in the day. If the majority of hours in a day must be exchanged for relatively low wages it is easy to get locked into an existence that requires every effort to simply survive. Our society provides aid and assistance in these situations. Hard-working people truly do deserve the benefits provided by programs society makes available to them.

✓ **For You and Your Organization**
Hard working lower-waged employees often qualify for public assistance programs funded by the country, state or federal governments. Because these programs are available to enhance workers' daily lives at no extra cost to your

business; simply letting workers know about available assistance programs can make a big difference in their lives and in the quality of work they can contribute to you.

Take It Away

> *"The welfare of each is bound up in the welfare of all."*
>
> *Helen Keller*

SECTION 5

Enhancing the Lives of Workers' Families

Food Assistance

What You Know

We live in a country of abundance. Warehouses and grocery stores are full of food accessible to those who can afford to buy it. But if you are not fortunate enough to be one of those, you will be among the many in our country that do not have enough food to eat.

For 1 in 6 Americans, hunger is a reality. Some people believe that the problems associated with hunger are confined to small pockets of society, certain areas of the country, or certain neighborhoods, but the reality is much different.

According to the USDA, in 2009 over 17 million children lived in households where unmet food needs were a daily occurrence. Health researchers have found that even mild under-nutrition experienced by young children during critical periods of growth impacts the behavior of children, their school performance, and their overall cognitive development. The problem affects the working poor as well as the unemployed. The significance of this problem for working mothers become even clearer when you learn the US Department of Labor consistently reports female-headed households are more than twice as likely than are male-headed households to be among the working poor.

Seniors are not exempt. In many cases, seniors who work full or part-time out of necessity must choose between purchasing needed medications and buying food.

Fortunately, our society recognizes that everyone deserves to eat. It's hard to raise a child, contribute to your community, or be a highly productive worker when you are hungry. That is why a number of public and private food assistance programs are already in existence. Some targeted populations of these programs include:

- ✓ The working poor
- ✓ Children
- ✓ Rural residents
- ✓ Suburban and Inner-city residents
- ✓ Senior citizens

The work is done, the programs already exist. The cost is taken care of. That means the only thing left to do is to get the benefits to those that deserve them. With the help of the internet it is a fairly easy to find the information you need. It takes time and it takes resourcefulness. These may be two characteristics you have, but like enough food to eat, many of your best workers may not.

WHY IT COUNTS

"I know its tough out there," said Faris, the office manager at Richard's Bookkeeping, "but our business is actually picking up. That's why I was glad to get your resume from the temp agency we use."

Faris was chatting with Katie, a new temporary worker.

"It's kind of crazy I guess. You know, I sacrificed, I went to community college," said Katie. "I mean I was never rolling in cash, but Marci and I made out O.K."

Katie was relaying to Faris that while she could never boast about living a luxurious life, the money she made as a pre-school math teacher had been enough to send her daughter, Marci, to an after-school program that the little girl's school ran.

Things drastically changed for Katie and her daughter a year ago when new management at her pre-school had been forced to make some budgetary cuts. Katie was left without a job and in need of affordable daycare as she submitted resumes and picked up temp jobs like the one with Faris.

"You know," said Faris, "when I was doing some looking into programs in Atlanta that could help our part-time staff, I ran across an after-school program that serves snacks and dinner to kids for a small fee each month."

"Really?" said Katie.

"Yes," replied Faris, "they keep their costs low due to the support and food they receive from the Atlanta Community Food Bank. No promises from me of course, but I'm pretty sure you would qualify. Let me go get that information for you."

While she waited for Faris to return, Katie started thinking that while she would still have to juggle the rent and utility bills, it would be great to know that Marci would have a nutritious meal each day after school was out and before Katie got home from work; . . . and that this support wouldn't cost her an arm and a leg.

1. Assume Katie's current income qualifies her for the program and Marci is ultimately enrolled. How do you think Katie's view toward her new employer will be affected? _____

   _____

2. Do you think Katie will actually perform better in her job with Richard's Bookkeeping Services knowing that her daughter is getting the food she needs? _____

   _____

3. Assume Katie shows real talent in her new job, is a terrific worker, and as a result is offered full-time employment with Richard's. Do you think Faris' efforts on behalf of Katie and her daughter would have any impact on Katie's decision to accept or not to accept the offer? _____

What To Do

Review the suggested low-cost activities below to determine if your own employees would benefit from them. If so, identify a target date for their implementation, then follow up to document your completion of the activity.

Suggested Management Activity	Target Date	Completion Date
• Research information about food assistance programs on the internet. Gather appropriate phone numbers, web-sites, addresses, and forms that might be necessary in completing applications for aid. WWW.FeedingAmerica.org is a good place to start your search.	____/____	____/____

- Elderly households are much less likely to receive help through the Supplemental Nutrition Assistance Program (SNAP) than non-elderly households, even when the benefits are the same. Encourage older workers to apply for these programs if they qualify.   ____/____   ____/____

- Research food assistance programs offered in your own state. Google *Health and Human Services* followed by the name of your state to begin the search.   ____/____   ____/____

- Check to see if your local school system participates in the Summer Food Service Program (a part of the Federal Government's National School Lunch Program). If so, obtain income eligibility guidelines and share them with staff whose children would qualify.   ____/____   ____/____

- Nearly every community has a chapter of the American Red Cross. The Red Cross operates food banks and soup kitchens across the country. Contact your local chapter to learn about the food aid programs they sponsor in your community.   ____/____   ____/____

- Contact the leader of your local church, synagogue, or mosque to learn about

religious-based food assistance programs
available in your area.   _____/_____   _____/_____

- Modify your new employee orientation
  program to add a component that informs
  new hires about food aid programs you have
  identified in your area and let them know
  who to contact for further information.   _____/_____   _____/_____

- Create a library of applications and contact
  information on-site. Make computer access
  available to your employees upon request, if
  possible.   _____/_____   _____/_____

WHY IT WORKS

✓ **For Your Employees**
It may be difficult for lower wage employees to research and understand the
various food assistance programs available to them. They may not have internet
access or writing and reading skills sufficient to complete the task on their own.
The strategy of trial and error may be their only hope. The problem with this
process is that it takes substantial amounts of time and can produce failure as
much or more than success. Help from you, along with some encouragement
refuting the negative stigma associated with food assistance, may be all they
need to get them to seek the aid they and their families deserve.

✓ **For You and Your Organization**
Once you have gathered all the information and understand the procedures
involved in food assistance programs you can catalogue the information and be
done with it. It takes the same effort to help one person or all of your employees.

By doing so, you can help keep them from hunger. Employees who are not worried about having enough to eat can be much more effective on the job.

Take It Away

> *"If you can't feed a hundred people, feed someone."*
>
> *Mother Teresa*

Child Care (daycare) Assistance

What You Know

People who are parents do not stop being parents when they get "on the job". Their responsibilities and loyalty to family remain and will most often take priority if the situation arises where they have to choose between what you need and what their family needs. And in most cases it should. As much as a person may want to be 100% devoted to their job responsibilities, conflicts between home life and work life often pop up. Since they are inevitable, you know that it makes good sense to attempt to minimize or possibly eliminate conflicts before they arise.

One of the biggest dilemmas is work/home schedule overlaps. Another is unexpected changes in these schedules. Let's face it, if everything in life went according to planned scheduling, everyone would be happy and life would be a lot easier. That isn't the case. Work life and home life are a constant juggling act. Given that fact, isn't it interesting that employers set work schedules and responsibilities in stone and seem shocked and perplexed when problems occur? Just holding employees to rigid expectations won't change or eliminate their home demands and won't guarantee their loyalty to the job.

If you can think outside the box and try to plan for these work/home clashes, it is possible to make their impact less troublesome. Most of the time it isn't the glitch that is the problem, it's the lack of planning to handle the change it creates that is the problem. The solution is flexibility, so:

⇒ Consider the possibility of varying work schedules if necessary according to employee personal needs.

⇒ Consider the option of reducing an employee to something less than 40 hours per week or 8 hours per day if that allows them to effectively combine their work/home demands.

⇒ Set-up job share arrangements for people who may benefit from that.

⇒ Coordinate situations which allow employees to assist each other with respect to family care.

⇒ Set-up child care onsite if possible.

⇒ Allow employees to make-up missed hours if possible.

⇒ Give incentives to employees to plan for conflicts before they arise rather than punish them for their personal needs.

WHY IT COUNTS

"Look, she wants to come in half an hour later than the other room attendants," said Jona, Executive Housekeeper at the Quality Courts All-Suite Hotel.

"I understand," replied Cindy Bowen the hotel's General Manager, "and that's why I'm saying no way."

"But Sylvia is one of my three best room attendants. Her daughter has been on the waiting list for the Head Start program for nearly 18 months," replied Jona.

"I get that she's having a tough time financially since her husband died in the accident, Jona. And I agree she's good. But all our room attendants start and leave at the same time. That builds teamwork and camaraderie among the housekeepers. You're gonna mess that up if you start showing favoritism to just one room attendant."

"Cindy, Sylvia didn't finish high school. She's determined her daughter will do better," replied Jona. "That's why she wants to get her in Head Start. They'll take her daughter for pre-school classes, give her access to health care screenings, referrals and follow-up support. They'll even help Sylvia apply for any social services they think she and her daughter might qualify for. In Arizona, the waiting list to get in is a long one. Jona's lucky her daughter got in. There are more than 10,000 kids still on the wait list."

"Look, I'm glad for her, but that doesn't affect the hotel" said Cindy.

"Well it affects me," said Jona, "because if she quits I'm gonna have to train another new housekeeper, and hope that she's half as good as Sylvia."

"You think she would really quit over this?" asked Cindy.

1. How do you think the guests at the Quality Courts All-Suite Hotel will be affected if Sylvia's request to start work late is granted? _____

    _____

    If it is not _____

2. As an employer, do you think the hotel "owes" Jona this schedule accommodation? _____

    Do you think Jona owes the hotel two weeks notice prior to her leaving?

    _____

3. Assume you were Sylvia. Would the opportunity to place your child in this program be great enough to make you seek a different job? _____

What To Do

Review the suggested low-cost activities below to determine if your own employees would benefit from them. If so, identify a target date for their implementation, then follow up to document your completion of the activity.

Suggested Management Activity	Target Date	Completion Date
Examine the possibility of setting schedules for certain employees to coordinate with their children's school days or other needs. This may require cutting weekly work hours or working split shifts. Adjust schedules and work hours according to the needs of the business and employees.	____/____	____/____
Hire 2 people for 1 job by creating job share for employees that are interested. Pair them to cover for each other during time-off situations such as illness, unexpected home demands, and vacations.	____/____	____/____
Stagger schedules for employees who could possibly share before and after school child care responsibilities.	____/____	____/____

- Create on-site child care if possible. Or allow temporary on-site child care to assist unexpected situations.   _____/_____   _____/_____

- Schedule for time off required for school issues, doctor visits, and the like by extending lunch hours or allowing partial day leaves to be "made up" in off hours.   _____/_____   _____/_____

- Be understanding about the need for flexibility. Encourage employees to anticipate the need for changes and work proactively to make the situation work in their best interest and yours.   _____/_____   _____/_____

- Take time to research day care opportunities in the area and make a list of options available to your employees.   _____/_____   _____/_____

WHY IT WORKS

✓ **For Your Employees**
CEOs of companies may be expected to almost give up their lives for their job responsibilities but lower wage workers shouldn't be. They have to struggle between loyalty to the job, the need for every penny of income and the care of their family. The luxury of fulfilling all of these responsibilities is priceless. Some adjustments at work and your understanding of their home scheduling conflicts can make that possible.

✓ **For You and Your Organization**

You are going to have to deal with the issues created by your employees work/home dynamics. You can scramble to react to the problems that will arise or you can actively plan and manage these situations. Being in control and having your company run smoothly is more likely with flexibility and preplanning because it is always better to act than react.

Take It Away

> *"What we do for ourselves dies with us.*
> *What we do for others and the world remains and is immortal."*
>
> *Albert Pine*

Accessing Housing Options

What You Know

Securing housing is not just the process of buying a house. It is likely that many lower wage employees don't have the means to buy a house, but they have every bit as much a need for "housing." Housing is any place a person has decided to or is required to live. It might involve owning or renting an individual dwelling, renting an apartment, renting a room, living with a parent/friend, being part of government assisted housing or even living in a hotel or motel.

Problems associated with housing may arise due to the difficulty to make payments, but they may also include working out issues with landlords, needing assistance with utilities, finding reputable repair contractors, controlling pests and insects, and more.

Accessing suitable housing may also be an issue that your employees are dealing with every day.

The issues and problems are likely to vary. Some you may be able to help with, but some you may not. Fortunately there are many organizations and government programs designed to give aid to those that need it and qualify for it.

Gathering the information on any available local, state or federal housing assistance programs that may be valuable to your employees is well worth your time and effort. It is almost impossible to concentrate and be dependable at work if you are having problems with housing. Housing related issues when children are involved magnifies the chaos and distraction. Your help in such situations can be invaluable to your employees and to their families.

WHY IT COUNTS

"Well, how did it go?" asked Dan Moss, the owner of Who Dat Novelties, one of New Orleans' largest providers of Mardi Gras beads, parade throws, masks and party decorations. Located in the downtown area of New Orleans, Who Dat also provided customers a wide variety of specialized products including school supplies, personalized cups, caps, pens, and other custom imprinted products.

"I guess I'm not sure" replied Frankie Allen. Frankie had been working at Who Dat for two years and was one of Dan's best. Customer orders were packed and shipped from the Who Dat warehouse where Frankie was employed as an order packer. And he was a good one.

It was for that reason that Dan had encouraged Frankie to go to the Armistead Apartments to fill out an application to get an apartment. Dan knew from attending the last meeting of his local business owners' association that Mike Breenan had just purchased and renovated the apartment complex. At the meeting Mike had made it a point to let the meeting attendees know that this company was actively trying to fill it.

Because the complex was located near the Who Dat warehouse, and because he knew the lower-income housing Frankie could afford was scarce near the warehouse, Dan had called the locale HUD office and confirmed that the complex had applied to accept Section 8 housing vouchers. In fact, willingness to accept section 8 voucher holders had been a condition of the county's approval for Brennan's company to get a five year property tax deferment on the complex after it was renovated.

Section 8 vouchers helped lower income workers like Frankie afford decent, safe, and sanitary housing in the private market. Since the assistance was provided on behalf of the family or individual, participants were able to find their own housing, including single-family homes, townhouses and apartments.

"When I called to make the appointment, they said they had lots of units to show me," continued Frankie "but when I got there and I told them I would be using a section 8 voucher, they said all the one-bedroom units like what I wanted were gone. That's when they said they would put me on the waiting list."

1. Why do you think Frankie was placed on the wait list instead of being offered an apartment? _____

2. Do you think low income workers face obstacles to securing safe and affordable housing that higher income workers do not face? _____

3. Assume you were Dan, would you be willing to make a direct call to Mike on Frankie's behalf? _____
   If so, what would you say _____
   _____

What To Do

Review the suggested low-cost activities below to determine if your own employees would benefit from them. If so, identify a target date for their implementation, then follow up to document your completion of the activity.

Suggested Management Activity	**Target Date**	**Completion Date**
• Research information on the internet. A good way to start is by typing "Low income housing assistance" followed by the name of your state, into your favorite search engine.	____/____	____/____
• Make available to your employees a list of habitat resale stores, charitable repair services, and temporary housing options, etc., they can access in case of emergency.	____/____	____/____
• Become aware of affordable housing within easy access of your location.	____/____	____/____
• Consider implementing a program to help employees find suitable roommates.	____/____	____/____
• Gather appropriate phone numbers, web-sites, addresses, and forms that might be necessary in completing housing assistance applications.	____/____	____/____

- Make the use of company computers available to your employees who need to use them to apply for housing program assistance.

_____/_____   _____/_____

WHY IT WORKS

✓ **For Your Employees**
Housing is as important as food for sustenance, but it is much more difficult to obtain and maintain. It is nearly impossible to function effectively in any area of life without stable housing. Everything else pales in comparison. However, once housing is secure an individual's focus easily switches to other things, adding to that person's ability to work and succeed.

✓ **For You and Your Organization**
One of the most valuable attributes of a good employee is dependability. The only way to expect that from an employee is when their basic necessities of life are fulfilled. The effort it takes to aid your employees in stabilizing their basic housing needs can change their lives and . . . yours!

Take It Away

> *"A house is a home when it shelters the body And comforts the soul."*
>
> *Phillip Moffitt*

Supporting Local School Systems

What You Know

Everyone dreams of making it big in America. But you know that for every person who realizes their "American Dream" and thus experiences enormous financial success, there are hundreds more that live their lives in a daily economic struggle to survive.

Working hard to get by in a lower-waged job may not be everyone's dream, but you also know that holding a steady job is much better than the alternative. Unemployed, homeless, living addicted, living with violence, spending time in prison and living without hope are the non-work alternative situations many unemployed persons face daily.

Not everyone can achieve a dream of great wealth, but everyone deserves a chance to live a life of peace, happiness and dignity. You don't need a lot of money to do that; but in America, education is the key to making it happen. In fact, an education gives everyone the opportunity to live life fully. Without it, a person's odds of properly caring for themselves or their families drop dramatically. That's why local schools and their efforts to reach students at the greatest risk of dropping out of school are so important and so needed.

The fact is, drop-outs are a growing problem in America. Nationwide it is reported that only 71 percent of all students graduate from high school and only about half of all Black and Latino students graduate. Of those who drop out, less than half will ever return to finish.

With studies showing increases in the number of students who aren't graduating, public officials are concerned those numbers will mean rising costs for social programs and prisons, as well as lost tax revenue because of the reduced earnings potential of drop-outs. Lower local, state, and national tax revenues are the most obvious consequence of higher drop-out rates. State and local economies suffer further when they have less-educated populaces, as they find it more difficult to attract new business investment. Simultaneously, these entities must spend more on social programs when their populations have lower educational levels.

Your personal connection with lower-wage employees gives you a unique and precious opportunity to get involved in your local school's student retention, or "Stay in School" programs.

These programs work and are of greatest importance to low-wage workers. That's because the children of these workers are those at the highest risk of dropping out of school. High school students from low-income families (the lowest 20 percent) are six times more likely to drop out than students from higher income families. Because that is true, your efforts in supporting your local school system's "Stay in School" programs can be, literally, "life changing," . . . one child at a time.

WHY IT COUNTS

"Thanks for meeting with me," said Trisha Sangus to Joshua Davidson.

Joshua was the owner of Three Men and Truck moving services. Joshua had started the company when he purchased a 14-foot truck for $500.00 and had hired a pair of movers to move the furniture and legal records of the area's largest law firm to its newly constructed offices across town.

He had built the company from the ground up and now, five years after it was started, it employed over 75 movers, truck drivers and clerical staff. Joshua had agreed to meet with Dr. Trisha Sangus, the superintendent of public schools for the city where Three Men and a Truck was located.

"You're welcome", replied Joshua, "but I have to tell you. I don't think our company is the kind you are looking for to join your 'School and Business Partnership' program."

"Why do you say that?" asked Trish.

"Well look, let's be realistic," said Joshua, "most of my employees are not going to be after school tutors in math or English, or most of your other subjects. And they aren't going to make class presentations. Don't get me wrong. They're great people. And very hard working. But I just don't see how I or my company could be of much help to you."

"Well," replied Trisha, "I do hope I can convince you to change your mind. In our district we have a special teacher recognition program where we identify and reward those teachers who our students say made the biggest impact on them staying in school. Once a year we honor them at an awards luncheon we hold at the Hilton downtown. It's a chance for us to publicly recognize the great work they do for our kids and for the future of our community. Being a sponsor for one teaching award is only $50.00. We provide lunch to the sponsor and use the rest to buy a small gift for the teacher. The Hilton picks up the lunch cost for the teachers selected, so we can use the entire $50.00 donation to pay for the sponsor's lunches and buy teacher gifts. Do you think Three Men and Truck could help us this year as an awards luncheon sponsor for our outstanding teachers?"

"How many teachers?" asked Joshua warily.

"Just one . . . plus as many more as you would like!" replied Trisha with a smile.

1. Do you think Joshua was likely aware of the school's awards program-related needs prior to meeting with Trisha? _____
2. Assume you were Joshua. Would you donate to the Teacher Awards Luncheon? _____
3. Do you think Joshua's business will be affected now, or in the future, by the quality of education offered in his city's public school system? _____ In what ways? _____

_____

What To Do

Review the suggested low-cost activities below to determine if your own employees would benefit from them. If so, identify a target date for their implementation, then follow up to document your completion of the activity.

	Target Date	**Completion Date**
Suggested Management Activity		

- Meet with your local school district superintendent and let him or her know about your interest in helping them achieve their district's student retention goals.   ____/____   ____/____

- Meet with your local school board President or board member(s) to let them know about your interest in helping achieve the district's educational goals.   ____/____   ____/____

- Encourage your local Chamber of Commerce, Rotary, Kiwanis or other area business associations of which you are a member to designate an individual to serve as liaison to your local school district to identify needs local businesses may be able to address.   ____/____   ____/____

- Stay informed about one-time events (fundraisers, community learning activities and the like) where your staff at all levels can volunteer their time and energy to help ensure the event's success.   ____/____   ____/____

- In partnership with school officials, devise a way to measure and recognize student success (for example, a company sponsored pizza party to reward good attendance).   ____/____   ____/____

- Volunteer yourself and seek the assistance
  of other qualified staff to act as tutors
  (for example in literacy, math, or health
  education) in schools that serve significant
  at-risk student populations.   ____/____   ____/____

WHY IT WORKS

✓ **For Your Employees**

All parents want the very best for their children. Their biggest wish is that their children are able to achieve more for themselves than they were able to achieve. Their biggest fear is that their children will fail at living their lives fully. In many cases, school systems serving large numbers of lower-income families struggle to maximize their use of scarce resources. In that way, they are very similar to families that struggle to help their children succeed in life. It truly does take a community to raise a child. Because that is true, your involvement in improving the educational opportunities of their children is one of the best things you can do for lower-waged workers.

✓ **For You and Your Organization**

Societies improve when their people are educated. Families function better, governments function better and business functions better. Employment and tax revenues rise. The economy improves, crime goes down and the need for social programs decreases. Most importantly, people live happier, healthier lives. And your business benefits as a result.

When you take steps to better your community's educational system, you are taking steps to make a better world for all.

Take It Away

"We cannot do great things on this Earth, only small things with great love."

Mother Teresa